# A Year in Shorts.



Mr E

ISBN: 1494801868
ISBN-13: 978-1494801861

For my lovely friend Justin, AKA, *Mr Da Silva*, Bangkok just wouldn't have been the same without you; maybe I should have called the book, "Paedos in Speedos?" Let's have many more giggles and adventures.

# CONTENTS

# ACKNOWLEDGMENTS

Inspirational texts:

"The Republic," by Plato, translated by Benjamin Jowett.
"A Moveable Feast," by Ernest Hemingway,
Essays and articles by Jonathan Kemp.
Jack Lothian for the cover magic.

I use a fake name purely for work reasons, to the people I care about, it's no big secret who I am. I am blessed with a wonderful support network.
MANY THANKS!
Friends and family at home and overseas, couldn't have done it without you. Massive love to Meriel and Andrew, Susie and Chris and Laura. Also, uncle Banks and aunty Jen, Melissa and Dazzy, Donna Dee, Eleeta, Lucy G (now Baker!) and the French boys.
Lisa (the Dame), James Browne, Mel, Libby, Damian, Maz, Claire and Becs and the Bristol crew. Thanks to Kit Hammonds at Publish and be damned for the support.
Declan, Tom, Chance (and Mole), Graham, Selina, Lizzie, Ria, Beth, Lucy, Mr Drifter, Aidy and the "I hate Bono and his fucking face," lovelies.
Thanks too to Martin and Uwern, from Out There magazine.
It wouldn't have been possible without the comments and criticisms of all those folk who followed the blogs.
Ms Fear, Mr Ampersant, and Mr Oriordan, I'm looking at you in particular, and not forgetting a proper *cheeky finger* for the mucky-talk with Hannah and auntie Georgette.
Big, no, HUGE hug to Sam in London for the concept.
Big hugs to all my new friends in Asia, particularly Jess and Jenny in Bangers. Big up to Chris in South Africa you are a love. Also Julie and Go and the Bar 23 lovelies, for boozy giggles, and a welcome respite from all the crazy paedos. Thanks to uncle Tony and P.Nala, Tent and 3rd, Simon and John for being my Bangkok family. Richard, I look forward to more Saturday coffees and letchings! Massive hug to Sam in Hong Kong for the holiday, and all the lovely boys I met in Taipei, Princess James, Chang, Po Fu and Ivan. Cheers to all the chaps at Babylon for the great times and wonderfully smutty memories.
There are so many friends and lovers I will thank in private, you know who you are. ;-)

# INTRODUCTION:

"If the reader prefers, this book may be regarded as fiction. But there is always the chance that such a book of fiction may throw some light on what has been written as fact." Ernest Hemingway.

Following a mid-life crisis of monumental proportions, I had decided to make many life changes. I drank way too much. That was the big problem. I also found that gay life in London was quickly leaving me behind. Traditional cruising grounds were becoming playing fields for an army of health obsessed antipodeans, and all of my gay friends were talking about house prices and the cost of civil ceremonies. I left my various jobs in the entertainment industry and I re-trained as a lecturer. I decided to move to Asia. A very close friend in London had encouraged me to begin a project where I would write a short essay every month in order to capture some of my experiences, I would then ask my friends for feedback in order to help improve my prose. So I started several blogs.

Inspired by Ernest Hemingway's wonderful, "A Moveable Feast," I wanted to capture an authentic sense of my experience.

It's not a linear narrative. Like a blog, I have presented each short story with the most recent first, so if you choose to read this in one sitting, you finish where I began the project, back in Dalston.

In writing each story, I have begun with real conversations or scenarios, I have then digressed into musings, memoirs and sensations triggered by these interactions. In many ways, even though the temporal sequencing is non-linear, it's a more authentic mapping of my experiences. The bullet points indicate that a quote is a recording of an actual statement or conversation that has taken place.

I have found with many of my writings that when I try to convey an objective truth, my prose reads like fiction, and in trying to convey a fiction, I have ended up revealing an underlying truth.

What I am left with, is a rather intimate portrayal of my personal growth, as well as a depiction of the interesting characters I have come across.

I question many aspects of my sexuality; however, this collection is not purely about *gayness*. I like sex, so I do present this aspect of my life in an explicit way, but it's more about the ridiculous aspects of life. Perhaps those who are easily offended might like to skip through parts, but if you do, I think you miss the point, swinging through the polarities makes life more interesting.

To some extent this is a self indulgent exercise, but for the majority of my waking life, I concentrate on the happiness of other people, so the whole project has been quite cathartic.

I have been particularly interested in documenting the voices of many of the drunken old queens that I have bumped into, they are quite fascinating people. It's not my intention to judge these men, or ridicule them, but sometimes they can be very difficult to be around, so their stories come across as quite uncomfortable. I don't wish to offend anyone, just paint the picture that I see.

Some of these stories read like impressionist paintings, they are vague, but I hope they capture something of the transience of modern life.

I have been fascinated by Plato's allegory of the cave, I feel it is responsible for many things, not all of them particularly healthy. I reference various translations in the text, particularly Benjamin Jowett's online translation, and to some extent Allan Bloom's translation. I do not quote these texts directly; however, they have worked their way into my ideas.

These are by no means complete narratives, there is no, "once upon a time," or, "happily ever after." They are a collection of characters and assumptions that exist in the moment.

With that in mind, I feel I should point out that I have, to some extent, embellished many of the characters who appear, they are subjective interpretations of people I have met along the way. Names have been changed to protect the guilty. Therefore any similarities to real people are purely coincidental.

# PART 12 – BANG KAPI – JULY - 2011

I had descended with some trepidation. It felt like I was looking for justice, but here in Bangkok there is no justice, only karma. The motorbike taxi driver who had greeted me at the entrance to my condo was particularly feral, he had skin tight jeans and oil stained hands. He reeked of Thai whiskey, cheap cigarettes and fingering. A heavy night weighed down on his eyelids, and I could see the morning sun was not his friend. He drove like a lunatic and decided to have an argument with a girl on his phone while we were speeding on the burning overpass.

Now I am sitting in a soulless shopping mall, listening to a fat, old drunk who is dressed like a clown. He is talking and all I can hope is that this grotesque scene is merely a shadow dancing on the wall of my imagination.

- "...You see it was the seventies and it was a whole different time back then..."

I'm not exactly sure why I had arranged this meeting with James, it is the third time that I have met him. I suppose I had become fascinated by the twisted turns of our conversations, I don't know, I have always been drawn to the macabre.

As he pours whiskey from his silver flask into his paper Starbucks cup, I am still trying to figure this all out.

He's talking again but I'm not really listening. I acknowledge the clangs of the dropping names which animate his anecdotes, but these people are meaningless to me. Who are they? It's a hollow list of notorious drunks who were all celebrated at some point for being, "such fun."

James Farnham is now both spiritually and physically redundant, he does little more than consume in order to maintain a veneer of usefulness. He looks like something that might have knocked up Ronald McDonald's mother at a traveling fair back in the 1960's. Beneath his rubber mask and bright orange wig, his thinning hair is dyed sandy brown in order to make him look younger. As he removes the mask and the wig to drink his coffee, I cannot help wondering where the wig ends and his hair begins. I think he likes people looking at him.

He absorbs attention along with everything else. From opulent furniture, to exotic liqueurs; from obscur objet d'art, to young looking boys; everything he hoards becomes indistinguishable. It seems obvious to me that he has replaced the draconian systems of his Mother's regime with a shambles of camp tat and ludicrous hair dye.

His Mother lingers.

60 years ago, James Farnham was born to a woman who had been raised by Indian servants in Calcutta. He has mentioned this fact many times. Using a dead woman to describe a 60 year old man seems very odd; however, it is clear that she is ever present in his thoughts. I can see with every artificial gesture he makes that he never questioned the ridiculousness of her etiquettes. I think she is the reason that he absorbs the world around him. Despite his bulky physique, every move betrays his mother's relentless insistence on efficiency and grace being the mark of civilized people. I'm guessing that he has never challenged these assumptions, and as a result, he has inherited a sense of responsibility to continue this warped pilgrimage of progress towards enlightenment. I think he has always seen himself as someone who matters. From what I can gather, his story is one of perceived revolution. In his mind the 60's had changed the world, so now he gets to dress like a clown and hang out with Thai children, just for fun.

On the 9th of April in 1969, while studying classics at Bristol university, James had witnessed the maiden flight of Concorde from Filton airfield. From our conversations it is clear that this is a symbolic moment in his life.

*Something about technology making the world a better place?*

Eventually I find out that he had also met his first wife, Elsie, at the airfield that day, but it was Concorde that had proved to be his most cherished memory. Elsie's a Welsh singer, a poor man's Dorothy Squires; so naturally I'm thinking she's a monumental drunk.

To sit in a Starbucks listening to James speak about the 1960's is oddly disturbing, because the deja vu is earth shattering. Not just for me, I'm sure that anyone else listening to him will have heard this story before.

Once upon a time the world was black and white and grey. Men wore dark suits and blank expressions and glasses which denoted rank. Women were known as, "girls," and they wore light grey dresses and spoke with received pronunciation. Everyone was disinfected with impeccable morals and a strong sense of social order.

One day, around 1963, young people discovered they could earn a fortune selling sex, drugs and rock and roll to each other. Then, as everyone knows, the world exploded into a colourful scene of sexually charged revolution and change; suddenly, the whole world was young and free and beautiful; well, according to James.

At some point in the conversation I am sure he has mentioned the phrase, "...and it felt like anything was possible." I find it hard that people still believe this story, yet it is clear James really does believe in his perpetual pilgrimage to a civilised utopia. The world would be a better place if only everyone listened to him.

Far from posing any real chance of accord, the old ideologies only exist in opposition to each other; they play out as circuses and we, in the audience, still hold our breaths for the flying man on the trapeze. James believes he changed the world, and presumably the world owes him a debt of gratitude. His unlimited credit fuels this sense of entitlement and at times, if he drinks enough, you can see the real matter of his wealth - the potential for violence and intimidation.

I am drifting in and out of the conversation, but it doesn't really matter, I've heard it all before.

Posh boys still sing the blues and romanticise about the struggles of the working man. Young girls still drink gin in order to forget that they have a say. The very notion of class war has been assimilated into the accepted norm. It's something we do when we're young. James talks of his formative struggles, his absent father and relative financial hardship, and uses these facts to underscore the empathy he presumes to have with everyone else. Maybe this is the key to his success; I mean, how else do men get to travel the world and think nothing of dressing as clowns just for fun?

This is all an act.

This is all a pantomime, and I can see right through it. He's pretending to be a poor man made good, even the ludicrous pretensions of his mannerisms are carefully concocted. He's a fraud and this eccentric facade is merely for the benefit of an audience. It is played out for my entertainment, and it is nothing more than a desperate attempt to appear controversial. Behind the smoke and mirrors, the big shoes and the striped pants, the struggles and the temptations, there is nothing.

At the university he had been a vocal advocate of Marx and the other Utopians. In Bristol he had been relatively poor and he had viewed his fellow students with envious eyes. On rainy days he would sit in Clifton, nursing a pint of tepid cider, and talk about the corruption of the ruling class. Then he graduated and went to work in slough. For James Farnham the sixties were over. University had taught him that it wasn't the subject you studied, but the narratives you weave that truly matter, he has fashioned a story that has come to define him.

- "...You see it was the seventies and it was a whole different time back then..."

And what about the 70's Mr Farnham?

Surely that was a halcyon time for grown men to dress like clowns and pedal paedophilia dragged-up as popular youth culture?

It would appear that during the seventies, James Farnham had lived a double life. By day he was a boring suburban suit, by night he was something of a local celebrity, apparently they were swingers, and Elsie was a notoriously outrageous hostess.

His work was far from exciting, but he took to it very well.

It was the first time that he had actually encountered the opinions of the working man, and he didn't like it at all. He was working as a middle manager in a factory that made underwear that he never bought. The factory was located in the Slough trading estate, him and Elsie settled in a beautiful new house nearby. James had welcomed village life in a would-be conurbation.

Though he is still incredibly shaken by his former workers; like his mother, they linger and he mentions them often. He frequently talks about his negotiations with the unions, he says he respected them, yet he couldn't understand them. Perhaps it was the accents? A lot of them were Polish, a fact that he recounts again and again presumably to highlight how cosmopolitan he is, but I think that he had never spoken to men like this before. They had talked of their rights and they hadn't just asked for more pay and better conditions - they had demanded it. He began to think of them as ungrateful dependents, and he learned to loathe them.

Thinking about it, whenever I have met James, he has spoken of the unions with a kind of vitriol that most people save for the Nazis. These rants are impassioned with the language that is employed to start revolutions or wars, and I suppose for James, this was his war. During our conversations it is clear that he has yet to reconcile this conflict in his mind, he sees it as a personal affront and he cannot understand the betrayal. After all, he had written many articles and attended many demonstrations to defend the rights of these working people - why were they so intent on holding civilisation to ransom?

I have noticed that when he speaks of his employees, he uses the pronouns, "they," and "them." In doing so, it is clear to me that he drew the lines years ago and has been at war ever since.

So, as a result, I always try and steer him away from talking about the seventies when he's been drinking; which means that I am always trying to steer him away from talking about the seventies.

It's lunchtime in a shopping mall and he is already starting to slur his words. He has been performing on stage with some children in a local beauty pageant. He has another show to do later this afternoon and I have to admit I really want to see it with my own eyes.

Tell me more about the seventies Mr Farnham.

He has previously informed me that he had employed the language of socialism in order to trick the unions into signing away their jobs. He had spoken of, "fairness," and "equality," while secretly, he was preparing to import cheaper labour; people from overseas, people who would be less concerned about pay and conditions. The plan had been successful and for his ingenuity, he was awarded with a promotion. If anyone objected to his tactic he labelled them a racist - thereby silencing any tangible opposition. In doing this, he had successfully subverted the term racism and eroded the concept beyond recognition; indeed, talking to him he is very conscious of this. He is not at all embarrassed about exploiting any divisions in order to maintain productivity and further his career. James climbed the career ladder and led the company towards an ever elusive concept of efficiency.

Eventually this required him to move production to Thailand, where people worked all day for less than the price of a Starbucks latte. The company has now moved to Amata, an industrial park to the east of Bangkok that seems desperate to manufacture a community. It's a lot quieter than Slough, less noise and more space. James likes it because he has 3 female personal staff who are beautiful and do everything he asks without question. He says they know their place.

I have become conscious that he has repeated himself several times, I can see the warning signs.

- "...Huhurgh Hurgh, Mmmwell, you see-of course-sit was the seventies you see, n'it was a *wHOOOOOOOOle* different time back then..."

His life in the seventies was one of deception.

He lived in a newly built house near Wexham with Elsie, and to many he was the embodiment of a happily married man. Behind the scenes, he tells me that he was incredibly promiscuous; he has spoken fondly of erotic encounters in public places. How much of this is actually true is unclear. However, the relish with which he describes frantic wanks while wedged against old porcelain soaked in piss certainly rings true. It's clear that in his booze addled mind he loved these encounters more than his wife. I can't say for sure, but I'm guessing one of the reasons that he married Elsie was that she was one of the few women with whom he felt comfortable lying. And I'm guessing that they were drunk a lot.

True, I am playing the omniscient narrator, I can only speculate on their marriage. I piece together the information given to me and embellish what lies in between. In my defense, I have spent many hours piecing through the fragments of memories and notes from my talks with James; because, frankly, she's a mystery. He's mentioned her many times, however she remains anonymous. I know the sketch of her character but nothing else. He also evades all of my attempts to elaborate on his son and his daughter by Elsie...

He tells me about the young looking boy who is fucking him now. He looks mischievous when he talks about this, occasionally he assumes a distanced glaze in his eyes that refuses to make contact with mine. He shifts his baulk in the low chair and ridiculously colourful suit, and I become aware that he is aroused just thinking about his lover.

I'm not sure if anyone has ever experienced talking to a semi aroused, drunken clown in a busy shopping mall before, as moments go, it's pretty awkward.

He is distracted and his eyes are searching for some stimulation and they come to rest upon the slender hips of our geeky-looking waiter. James' eyelids squint a gluttonous moment of gratification, and in a hideously Freudian moment, his conversation ambles towards obscenity as he recounts the tales of his new lover's sexual exploits.

- "I love to feel his rock-hard cock inside me..."

I try very hard not to care, or even to let his words take effect, but there is something primal in imagining true horror. Already my overactive imagination has concocted a revolting picture of smooth, tanned skin greedily exploring the folds of James' over-indulged rump. I bulk at the thought of his muscle-weak corpulence receiving the attention and the care of anyone, but why should I care? My prissy judgement says more about me than it does about him.

It strikes me that I am being hypocritical about this. In asking myself the question, "*why would anyone share such intimate information with virtual strangers?*" The irony is not lost on me. I have looked back at my own blogs, postings and articles, and I cannot fully understand my motivations for discussing my sexuality. Is it pure narcissism? Is it indulgence? I've not ruled these explanations out; however, I maintain that human sexuality is a natural aspect of our lives that frequently gets distorted.

I feel to some degree that my sexuality has been hijacked. I'm not sure of the exact moment it happened, but all of a sudden, I felt the language of gay discourse no longer included me. It began to serve a privileged elite who publicly proclaimed their love and sought to marginalize the cruising that has, at its heart, an authentic engagement with the sexuality of men. Being gay for me isn't about Conran interiors and tasteful soft furnishings, it's about sucking cock.

We maintain that discussing our sexualities in public forums is vulgar, yet in silencing these aspects of our character we endure many disruptions to our daily lives.

That being said, it would be disingenuous of me to deny that I too have noticed the slender waist of the geeky waiter. If I am being completely honest I register his physique and in a moment I picture a passionate coupling and I taste the salt of his sweat and feel the coarseness of his hair between my lips. I suppose the only difference in this moment between James and myself is that I do not vocalise the fantasy.

- "I was married for over 10 years, so now I've decided to follow the path of least resistance."

I have heard this line repeated many times before. It always precedes a lengthy, intimate description of his relish at fucking young looking Thai boys, all of whom have no agency in the narrative.

When James describes his new lover to me, it is a fractured image. It is compartmentalised beyond all recognition. It is a picture comprising of, "*large hands,*" "*strong arms,*" and of course a, "*long, thick cock.*" I piece these things together in my mind and cannot see the person. I see a jumble of stereotypes and cliches that do not settle into anything other than a broken picture of subjective assumptions.

"...He's 17 but he looks much younger, I just wanted to have some fun, I wasn't looking for love or anything, he seduced me..." The thing with James is that he will never profess to seeking anyone's approval, and yet at this moment this is exactly what he is doing. It's almost as if he sees me as some kind of moral judge and jury, like I am the unspoken voice of his past conscience. The really sad thing is I don't care what he does.

- "...It's not about the money or anything; no, of course I give him 2000 a week for his clothes and things so he looks nice, no, it's not about the money, it's about the fun... He really makes me laugh you see..."

And then it happens, I become aware of the fact that he is no longer talking to me, he is conducting a conversation with something else, something that is not in the here and now. He is justifying his actions to a memory.

. . . . . . . . . . . . . . .

In Thailand I have been lucky enough to witness many bizarre things, a lot of which, people in the UK might find very odd. I have witnessed my class of teenage boys, dress up as girls, and erotically dance to *Lady GaGa* songs for the entertainment of a visiting football team. I have sat in the studio of a televised singing competition and watched young Thai teenagers dress up as children and erotically dance to the applause of their families. I'm going to go out on a limb here and propose that the sexualisation of young people is not traditionally frowned upon. Indeed, many conversations I have with different people here would indicate that sexuality is frequently identified with youth.

If you are shocked by the notion that over sexualising young people is pretty normal, then you need look no further than our own western popular youth culture. The sexual liberation with all the fun of the teenage party is intrinsically linked to our consumption. We consume the enthusiasm of youth and subvert it into an endless popularity contest. Cool is a currency that nobody can ever really cash in, look at the pictures of a 15 year old Kate Moss or Britney Spears – it's sex. If you're looking at the work of Terry Richardson, for example, the hipster liberals will completely fetishise young looking naked girls, particularly those who will have sex with sleazy old photographers. We may loathe men like Terry Richardson, but they certainly hold a mirror up to some men's sexuality.

Perhaps this is all down to the people like James, the pioneers of our beloved sixties revolution.

So watching James, wearing a pair of oversized, striped dungarees and a rubber mask that is the stuff of snuff porn, bouncing around a stage in a shopping mall is really not as disturbing as it seems when I type it. In fact even as the young Thai kids, over dressed in sexy teenage fashion, get up and start dancing with him, I don't feel in the slightest bit unsettled. To be honest their parents couldn't be more proud. It reminds me of those times in the UK when parents used to send their children on to shows like, "*Jim'll' fix it,*" and "*Top of the pops.*" Wasn't that the 70's? Seriously, is there anything more obviously wrong in the world than Jimi Saville's tracksuit? Perhaps it was a whole different time back then.

- "The boy is on his way now..."

James is drunk and he is beginning to frighten me. He is reaching that moment of equilibrium that precedes the flip into madness. It is the time when he expresses a sober piece of factual information. It's at that point I know he has had too much to drink. It is a statement that is devoid of all nostalgia and artifice, it is a tangible piece of information that signals a spiral into the horrific reality of his existence. It's almost as if James reaches the point where he becomes aware of his own ridiculousness and all pretensions aside, he sees himself as the drunken old queen dressed as a clown.

He looks beyond me and talks to the voices in his own head.

- "The thing about being a professional actor in Thailand is that nobody ever really takes you very seriously..."

He shifts in the seat and sways the booze filled latte from side to side. His chins judder in my general direction and emphasise his discomfort, he is sweating and his hair dye is running down the back of his neck.

- "They just think I'm some sort of fucking joke, I used to know Cary Grant you know, and here I am being a fucking children's entertainer!"

To be fair to James, even though his voice is raised, there are no children around who can understand what he is saying. Also, in the presence of the children, he is genuinely well behaved. There is something quite comforting in the way he gently interacts with them, I would say that there is nothing more traditionally English than a drunken old clown making children laugh. I find nothing inappropriate about his contact with the children. What does concern me, is that I am not a child, and therefore I am a legitimate target for his twisted drunken madness. He is riddled with whiskey and unfulfilled ambition, I have to keep telling myself that he isn't really talking to me.

His change of mood is instantaneous.

Unknowingly I have provoked him, he leans forward in short controlled jabs and spits his words at me as if they were back-handed slaps.

"...I just want a laugh, don't you understand that? I just want some fun... You're too fucking boring... My boy likes to have fun..." His face has contorted into a mask of rage and his words have lost their charm and been transformed into a venomous strike of contempt.

"... You think you're so much better than me, but you're boring... Sitting there with your fucking green tea! You can't judge me, who the fuck do you think you are?" I try to placate him as best I can, I am used to these outbursts from him, they are vicious and filled with rage, but they are never really directed at me. They are directed at his conscience.

- "...Tha's the trouble with all you European boys, all think you're someone special, well you're not. You're nobody, you're just fucking boring, I don't have to put up with all your shit, Asian boys are much more fun, they know a good thing when they see it..."

It is at this moment that his eye is caught by a smiling young boy who is walking towards the cafe. The boy looks so young and content. He looks like a young teenager, barely 14 years old, yet he moves with a self confidence that tells me he is most definitely older. He reaches out and tenderly places a hand on James's shoulder. I do not recognise him from the description that James had given me, but it would appear that this is the boy with big hands and a "*long, thick cock.*" Call me crazy, but I just don't get the attraction at all, what is the glue between these two people? Is it just about the money?

"It's time to go Mister, you drunk." It's odd to see someone so young have power over someone so angry. It is instantly clear that he has re-negotiated this afternoon's performance, I'm pleased about that, the thought of James being on stage in this state is truly frightening.

- "Ah yes, thank heavens you're here, you're such a good boy, this chap over here is becoming a bore."

He shakes the back of his hand in my direction. "I deal with people like you everyday, you're all full of shit, if you ever came for a job at my company then you wouldn't get it, that's the problem with people like you, you're all full of shit!"

He leaves without paying his bill and so I end up reluctantly buying his lunch. As I watch him wobble off being assisted by a teenage boy, I can't help feeling sorry for him. The initial shock of his verbal attacks has worn off and I feel sad that life can be so cruel. He doesn't even get to fulfill his obligations as a clown. James has been trained to rule the world and it's a world that no longer needs him.

. . . . . . . . . . . . . .

Like many Europeans, I was born to question the world around me. I inherited an inquisitive nature that tempted my forefathers out from the imprisonment of a metaphorical cave and into the sunlight. From an early age I wanted to know the form behind the shadow. This has always been a most treacherous and lonely path, it is a journey towards enlightenment that has no rational meaning. I see in James something akin to this, we share a common root despite our differences. Beneath the boozy, lecherous persona, James wants to strive out into the world and bring a rational order to the chaos. So consumed by his own self righteous motives, he cannot concede to the meaninglessness of his enterprise.

Indeed, where has this inquisitiveness brought any of us?

We have become a desperate diaspora of Morriseys and Cowells, a civilisation that points our fingers at the world and criticises everything and anything, while ignoring the fact that our time is over. It doesn't occur to us that we come across as clowns, spouting our stories of reasonable order while instigating pandemonium.

We learn everything and nothing, so our missionaries travel the world speaking of a universal peace, and our armies look for nothing but war. Is it any wonder that we in the west are frequently misunderstood?

I see in James the logical end to every pilgrimage, it is a promised land with two faces. One is jovial and fun, the other is vicious and cruel.

# PART 11 – LUMPINI PARK – JUNE – 2011

Standing in the dusky stillness of Lumpini park; surrounded by carefully trimmed shadows, it is difficult to imagine what avenues of undiscovered pleasure there are left for me to explore. The luxurious opulence of Thanon Ratchadamri and Rama IV slither off into the distance; they mate somewhere with my home road Sukhumvit, it is an unnatural coupling.

On these grand streets I have sipped champagne and languished in the company of some of the most beautiful people in the world. I dined with royalty.

From these towering boulevards radiate the stinking Sois; where I scuttled through rat infested homes that offered me sanctuary for 500 baht an hour.

But here, in the majestic Lumpini park, I contemplate the finer things in life.

I look out at the most awesome sunset. All around, the creatures that are quite alien to me stir. The monitor lizards, some as long as me, gently crocodile past and snake into the water with a slovenly 'plop'. Their laziness is deceptive and they disguise their speed with stealth – such cunning! My companion informs me, "they taste like chicken." It's hard to imagine such ancient beasts as food; but then, it would appear that everything can be eaten in Thailand.

My companion is ridiculously handsome. He is Thai and has the most beguiling features. His name, I think, is Noo. I have told him that my name is Jack, a lie of course, but then deception is the fabric of this town. He is dark and has a profile that should be carved in stone. He should be a statue standing somewhere sacred, and sands of time should gently lap him, and pay homage to his form.

His full lips have a natural propensity to pout, which gives you an indication of his temperament. He displays an odd mixture of aggressive rudeness and passive submission. At times he is bitchy and full of spite, other times he is unbelievably fragile. Such inconsistencies in his character make him both repulsive and alluring.

He has been feverishly busy with his task and takes a break to look at me.

"You always dress smart like this?"

"Indeed," I smile and stroke his ear-lobe lazily.

"I consider myself a cultural ambassador. I wouldn't want to do anything to let the side down."

He nods in agreement.

"Where your children live? London?"

"I don't have a family Noo. I hate the idea of having to love somebody and not have a choice in the matter."

He looks at me in disgust. As a bar boy he is probably distrustful of farrang, but what does he expect? He is clearly duplicitous in his affairs.

- "You should have family. Every man should have family...You are not man if you do not family...I will have many beautiful children."

The setting sun splashes a myriad of indescribable colours across the sky and I begin to feel quite lost. Joggers shuffle past, and their shapes become a strange silhouette slinking off into the darkness.

Bangkok is beautiful.

I am relaxed enough to consider Noo's words carefully, I always did have a tendency to procrastinate, does virility make a man? I suppose reproduction is our main purpose in life. To be fruitful is to be good, if you conveniently ignore the population crisis, and I am not fruitful.

It's an embarrassing thing to be forced to question your virility. Here I am in Lumpini park, surrounded by so much blossoming colour and life, and suddenly I feel quite barren. It is also an odd thing to have your virility questioned by a soi 4 bar boy; a man who has just spent the last 20 minutes sucking your cock...

. . . . . . . . . . . . .

It was like we had accidentally been transported to the 1970's and become contestants on a foreign game-show. The set was amazingly camp, it should have been in technicolour. We were unsure of the exact rules of the game; however, it was clear that we gave money, handed out flowers, and suddenly there was applause.

My friend assures me, there was a halcyon moment when I was set adrift in a sea of the most beautiful ladyboys. It was what heaven would be like if people with a sense of humour were left in charge. Not clinical, white or angelic, but blooming with colour and life. I was carried on a wave of transgender pilgrims. I handed out roses like a modern day prophet of wrong.

So began my Christmas affair with a mental ladyboy called Nina.

It is fair to say that her name wasn't the only thing about her that wasn't real. Despite my love of authenticity, I fell for her instantly. Unlike the other lady boys who try so hard to affect all of the mannerisms of bar-girls, Nina was androgynous and truly rock and roll. Her face was boyish and pretty and she had the body of a racehorse; she was like a Thai Grace Jones. She had a tattoo that slithered around her firm, slender form that was full of opulent dragons and oriental swirls.

Ladyboys generally take their inspiration of femininity from contemporary media. It's all about long hair and big-boobs and short skirts. They fulfill a highly masculine ideal of sexuality. Not Nina. She had short, cropped, feathered hair and wore kitsch outfits like some cool art-school rockabilly chick. Her performance was not just drag, it was an undulating wave of sexuality and fun. She was a rock star.

Being at the time somewhat naive about Thai bureaucracy, I had to go to Kuala Lumpur for a work permit. It proved to be a completely pointless and expensive exercise. However, it taught me never to listen to the Thai immigration help desk. Essentially, I was going to have to spend the christmas period in Bangkok, alone.

It was a particularly hot and humid Christmas eve and I had been working out at the gym listening to *Guns and Roses*. I'm not sure why, but they always make me feel quite festive; it's the nostalgia I suppose. Suddenly I discovered an unknown number in my phone. It was Nina. Within hours I was on the back of a motorbike taxi screaming up the Sukhumvit road, heading to meet her for a drink.

She was as beautiful as I had remembered.

It was like she had arrived from another planet, one that was completely detached from our own. A planet where gender was a game and the rules were yet to be made.

We drank through bars adorned with tinsel and cheery Thai people who shouted, "Melly Clistmas!" The street bars were devoid of most of the regular ex-pats; they had escaped to the islands for Christmas by the sea. It was like the city was made exclusively for our pleasure. We played and we danced.

The next morning, a blazing sun chased the sound of the bells from the temple into my room. It was Christmas day. Through a dry lipped hangover, I turned to look at my girlfriend in her slumber. She was contented and lay across my bed; stretched out, even in her sleep her limbs explored the world around her and tested every boundary.

Her breasts, though false, looked so natural and real, not too big. They graciously complemented her luscious form, and lying in my bed she seemed so complete. She was a whole person. I was forced to question my own masculinity, was I more or less of a man than her? Her truly beautiful body was not particularly masculine or feminine; but it could have been either. Her skin was a subtle mocha colour that was smooth and supple...

Nina you are a pioneer.
Your map a new perspective and it's tattooed on your back
For me to trace, and on your perfect face,
Your perfect face,
I can place a woman or a man,
In supple nights on satin sheets,
Dripping sweat that begs me to ejaculate the words,
"So hear me God!
Deny us and be damned."

I believe there should come a time in every mans life when he looks at his girlfriend, one Christmas morning and realises that her penis is bigger than his.

. . . . . . . . . . . . . .

As men, we often utilise the language of pioneers when relaying our sexual conquests. Everywhere men brag about who they have fucked and how this, "act," was achieved. It is an aggressive language. It is the language of rape. Men all over the world have a problem with getting fucked. Even on the gay scene, men define themselves by penetration: They are "passive," "active," "kings" or "queens." Yes, even homosexual activities are atomised and labeled into obscurity. You're not just, "gay," anymore; you're a, "white, Straight acting, non-scene, rice queen, bottom," whatever that means. I find the excesses of profiling and labeling completely unnecessary and boring. Such information sucks the fun out of every sexual encounter. Why not try something new? I have always liked to experiment.

Such was my affair with Nina, sex with her was like playing with Lego for the first time; you had to figure out which bits were going where. It was a case of something for everyone, not just, "business up top, party down below!"

You realise just how beautiful people are when they finally say goodbye. I lost Nina, as I had found her, in a crowd of people dancing.

It was New years eve, and I had spent a week with her laughing and loving. I had decided to treat us both to a 5 star Bangkok experience. You can afford to be extravagant in Bangkok, especially when you are English. £40 for an 8 course meal by the river is more than acceptable, and for my girl, well, let's just say I'm no cheap-skate.

The thing is, people who can afford a 5 star new years meal in Bangkok aren't that much fun to be around.

This quickly became apparent when my girlfriend arrived ripped to the (fake) tits on vodka and crystal meth. She looked stunning in her mini-dress, like some kind of beat chick from a cool, sixties art flick. Needless to say we were the best looking people there, apart from the staff, and we were definitely the most fun. It seemed we were the entertainment. Bored couples, full of bitterness, surrounded us in silence. All the money in the world and zero fun. What is the point of that?

By the time the delicious basil sorbet had arrived to "cleanse the pallet," Nina had flashed one of her boobs.

By the time the fish main course had arrived, Nina had dropped her fork, and while bending down to collect it, she had inadvertently given the table next to us a birds eye view of her hormonally shrunken testicles.

It's times like these that I am quite proud to be a country liberal. There is something quite satisfying about deconstructing the sour pretensions of a bunch of joyless straights. I never thought that I would ever get to say the words; "darling please, can you put your cock away until later? You're scaring the straights."

I made insincere apologies for her behaviour, and told the table next to us that she had just recovered from a nasty bout of ovarian cancer; the medication was making her ill. They were genuinely sympathetic which made it all the more ludicrous. I then asked for the bill, tipped handsomely and asked where I should take my inebriated guest.

Dancing in the streets of Silom it was, and what an unbelievably refreshing experience that is, to dance in the streets with someone so unaffected and beautiful. Even though she was false, created by a surgeon's knife, Nina was the truest person I encountered that night. She was what she was.

Then I lost her.

She said, "goodbye," and I knew our time was done.

I think of her fondly to this day. I hope that she finds that place where she belongs. Not the 5 star drab, or the gutter-soi grime; no, she belongs somewhere else.

. . . . . . . . . . . . .

Jimmy was from Plymouth and he said,

- "Why can't things be like they were? Men were men and women were women? You never know where you stand anymore, gays and lefty-Trotskyites have taken over the world..."

After I had heard him repeat the sentence for the tenth time, I realized that we had nothing at all in common, other than our west-country roots. Expats make the most obscure acquaintances; we are forced to look for something vaguely familiar. Thai people can be incredibly racist; to them, we are just ferrang and we learn to deal with it. Having said that, Jimmy was a particularly stupid cunt. He was one of those men who completely fails to recognise his own glaring hypocrisies.

- "Yeah, I moved here 10 years ago coz of all the immigrants taking over Plymouth. Too many blacks and Muslims for me, tha's why I like it here so much, they don't let 'em in..."

The fact that he was an illegal immigrant in Thailand had completely escaped him. In Jimmy's world he was entitled to live anywhere; not enjoy it, and maintain that wherever it was, it was worse than Plymouth.

What did I expect? I was in an Irish theme pub with a man who ordered nothing but steak and chips, and then moaned about how "shit" it was.

- "I dunno why, but they can't never cook chips proper here..."

When I was younger, I would have taken the time to reason with a man like Jimmy; possibly even talked him around, but these days, I can't be bothered. I let him prattle on, mainly in the hope that he would burst out laughing and reveal that this was all a piss poor gag.

I decided to wind him up a bit.

A scary thing to do considering Jimmy was massive, thick as shit, and he really liked fighting. I still maintain that, camp as I am, I show no fear. I have booted bigger boys than Jimmy out of my bed on a Sunday morning.

What can I say? I'm a country boy at heart.

"So, how do you find the Thai people?" I ask rather coyly.

"They hate us. All of us. They're stupid you see, they can't speak English."

I lean into the bar and politely motion for my bill,

"Do you speak Thai?"

"What me?" He laughs, "that rubbish? No. That ain't a language it's a load of stupid sounds. No, I don't bother with it, end'a'tha'day, you don't need it, they all speak English..."

I laughed and it was taken to be a friendly gesture. Perhaps to Jimmy I was some kind of kindred spirit.

Just then I was saved by the sound of Mercury.

"Don't stop me now," began with it's grandiose piano and suddenly I felt refreshed.

I hope that if there is a God, then he is somewhere, surrounded by poetry and porn; and he is being serenaded by Freddy Mercury.

Jimmy looked at me all bleary eyed and sullen.

- "I fuckin' love this song, Freddy Mercury, what a fuckin' legend. You know they all want us to think he's a bender now don't you?"
- "What, Freddy Mercury? Gay?"

I sounded so surprised! I had momentarily forgotten the fact that I was with a man who didn't get the joke.

- "Yeah... All those Trotskyites now want us to believe that Freddy Mercury was a poofter! It's the media you see, they're all run by fuckin poofters. My mate told me he died of cancer, all that AIDS stuff was made up."

I couldn't help thinking that I was responsible for this. If I had had children, perhaps – just perhaps, there would be less Jimmies in the world, but then again, who would murder all the puritanical bores? I decided to speak, if only for my own entertainment.

- "Yeah... He didn't make it easy for himself, being in a band called, "Queen," and fucking all those rent boys."

Jimmy was physically handsome and had a certain mindless charm. He looked at me with the most pitiable ignorance; which, I must confess, was rather arousing.

- "Yeah I know; still, even if he was a poofter he made the best songs, at least he wasn't a black. So, Jack... D'you wanna come back to mine?"

It was then that I noticed his hand was on my thigh; a large, over-manicured hand. It crept up my thigh to my crotch like an insect. He looked at me with the sorriest of eyes; they were the eyes of a desperate man. He was pleading for something.

I knew that look.

He wanted me, a fresh faced man from home, to tell him that everything was alright. He wanted me to stroke him and tell him that yes, he was a good boy, it was everyone else in the world that was to blame. He was looking for guidance. Perhaps I had given the same look to Nina? I grimace at the thought. I had nothing to give him but contempt. I left him alone at the bar.

. . . . . . . . . . . . . .

For just a moment Noo rests his beautiful ear on my chest. I leisurely fondle the shaved sides of his head as we sit and look at the darkening water. Here we are; two men, separated by cultures, years and languages. We are sharing a moment of tenderness in the dusk.

By the waters edge the monitor lizards suddenly scatter and there is an almighty splash. It is accompanied by shouting and policemen are by the waters edge with torches. I can just about make out their frantic gestures.

"What's going on?" I ask, my miserable grasp of Thai is a constant frustration to me.

"Oh... It nothing. Some bad people."

Through the undulating searchlights I make out the figures of two men who are soaking wet. They are being dragged from the water and beaten. Such violence in somewhere so peaceful seems outrageous; I am quite stunned. Here is the ferocious side of man. Here is the animal.

How does the saying go? Give a man a fish and he will eat for a day, but give a man a stick and he will batter everyone else and steal their fish? Something like that anyway.

Coughing up water and gasping for air; the men are chained in shackles. They are surrounded by security and soldiers, who use batons and truncheons to bludgeon the un-armed men as they flounder on the grass. For some strange reason, I am reminded of the opening scene of the film, "2001 - a space Odyssey."

The men surrender silently, and they are kicked towards the police station located in the centre of the park. Where they thought they were going to swim in a sealed lake, I do not know. It is an act that screams of desperation.

"Red shirt," says Noo.

I suddenly feel even more sterile. None of this is my business. In this matter I am an impotent observer. I think I am not alone, Noo gently rubs his face against my chest. It is a sympathetic gesture, one that is quite comforting, and this time he is alarmingly tender.

"I think that is another reason why I don't want a family," I say without thinking.

I arrange my clothes and step out from behind the picnic tables. We have rinsed the day of it's sunlight and now we are left with the darkness. Who can blame us for wringing every second of loveless gratification from the day, when all we have left are the shadows?

Noo adjusts himself and stands; even in the gloom, I can trace his perfect form.

"The bar open. I go. Come for beer?"

We move among the un-lit tables, and make our way out onto the road which bristles with people in track-suits.

I am numbed. It all seems so bizarre. What sort of world do we live in? It is obscene to think of men pleasuring themselves in a public park; yet it is perfectly acceptable for men to beat each other senseless. I curse my dandy dawdling. I should have done something; indeed, men have fought for less. I feel redundant.

We walk towards a neon sanctuary of drunken eccentricity; to Silom, the gleaming face of Bangkok.

Noo and I.

Two men separated by age, life and experience. Two men who committed a crime, yet witnessed such legitimate savagery from the sidelines. Therein lies the guilt.

We head to a place where life and laughter flicker without remorse.

In Lumpini park I had lost my bravery, that was the root of my shame. I momentarily sympathise with Jimmy; at least he would have done something reckless, something stupid, something manly. I was left feeling emasculated by what I had seen, not by what I had done. Does that make me less of a man?

# PART 10 - PETCHBURI - MAY – 2011

## FUCKING THREE WAYS:

One of my favourite restaurants back in east London was *"Les Trois Garcons,"* I was lucky enough to eat there several times, and I often wonder what it was that made me love it so much. Was it the richness of the food, the opulence of the design (I've always had a soft spot for stuffed animals wearing tiaras) or the slightly too cool for school staff? No, it was the fact that you sit in the uber-camp lounge of what is essentially a big gay 3 way. You're basically the filling in the physical manifestation of their spit roast.

It isn't the fantasy of a perpetual daisy chain that enthralls me, I betray my working class roots here, but it's the peculiarities of the day-to-day life that I still find fascinating. How does it work? Do they nag in stereo? Will their collective mid-life crisis result in an ever-expanding wardrobe of inappropriately tight disco wear? Perhaps a 3 way would be more stable than a less conventional twosome, who knows? Maybe I was looking for answers to my own inabilities to connect in a relationship?

I recently met 3 men in Bangkok who had been in a relationship for over a year. We met in a bar in Silom and they asked me where to go dancing. I told them DJ station, where else, and they asked me to join them.

They were from Moscow and they were painfully trendy and undeniably cute. They wore skimpy white shorts and tight T-shirts. For some reason they had all decided to wear matching Mr Spock/elf ears, which contrived to make them appear all the more fabulous. They swaggered through the club, seemingly oblivious to all the attention, in a way that only beautiful men in their twenties can when consumed with the solemnities of their love.

I got talking to Alex (the one with the glasses) who spoke English, he told me the history of their relationship and I was - how can I say - both fascinated and horrified. It was just so full on, heightened no doubt by the fact that they were all high. DJ station had closed, and while Alex recounted their passionately mental love story, the cleaning lady waddled past, moping up stale homo-piss from the toilet floor beneath our feet.

- "Sawaddeeee KAAAAAAAAAAAAAAaaaaaaaaaaaaah!"

She made it last 6 seconds, I counted.

On our way to GOD, Alex asked me if I had ever had a relationship with more than one man. I told him I hadn't had a serious relationship with anyone. I was not going to compete with the bonkers tale of his *oh so fashionably experimental* love affair; so, what was I meant to say? I just told the truth...

The week before meeting Alex and his fiances - yes, they planned on getting married somewhere - I had gone into the office on a Saturday to do some preparation. My secretary was slopping around the office, wearing his pink, furry slippers and playing computer games.

I was busy photocopying documents, generally doing his job, when the office phone rang and he answered like this:

- "HellaaaaaaaawW - krap, - s'wadeeee kraaaaaaaaaaaaaaaaaaaaahhhhhhp - Awwww jing Lor! - Loooor - AwwwwwwwwWWWWwwwww - Jing Lor - UUUuuurgh - chai - UUUrgh – chai - Krap - 'Wadeeeeee KraAAAaAAaaAAAaaaaaaaap."

He sniffed, hung up, and shoved a piece of fried pork in his mouth:

- "Who was that?" I asked,
- " She - not – say. She - Want - talk - wit – you. I - tell - heem - you – vely - busy."
- " Remind me again which university you graduated from with a first in business English? Was it a "he" or a "she" who called?"
- " It - man - call - I tell - her - you - call - back."
- " But, I am here!"
- "CHAAaaAaaaaaai. yes - YES - you - vely - busy - man. I - tell him - call - back. It - you - boyfLiend - from – Babylon."

I'm not making this up, he really does talk like this. It's like I'm living in a slightly racist sitcom from the 1970's. He bleats out words like a big, gay, asian sheep and I'm not sure of the power relationship here, but I'm convinced that I'm the boss in name only.

He has a point though, I do love Babylon.

If you are ever in Bangkok and you want to be the slutty filling in a real spit roast - and who doesn't? Then I can strongly recommend that you take a trip to Babylon sauna and resort In Bangkok's rich Sathon district. It's a great place to play and experiment with all kinds of weird and wonderful group stuff. I'm not sure why, but it has such a bad reputation among the Thai boys, they've all been of course, but emphatically deny it.

It is the only place on earth I can think of, where you can get felt up by a wealthy CEO from Hong Kong to the sound of Gustav Holtz's "Uranus;" which, by all accounts, makes it the very definition of, "*gay*."

My secretary had this to say:

- "Sauna - not - good - If - you - go - sauna - Bhudda - say - it - bad."

The fact that he spends all day conning gifts out of deluded lovers, makes me question his grip on Buddhist morality.

- "What's wrong with going to a sauna if you are a single man?"
- "Sauna - for - BAD - people - ghost - NOT - LIKE - men - go sauna."
- "Ghost?"
- "Chaaaaaaaiiiiiii Mister - *sniff* - Ghost."
- "What? Like Patrick Swayze? Or Casper? Anyway, I saw you at Babylon, remember? You were kissing that gormless man from Belgium."
- "HE - NOT - FROM - BELGIUMLAND - HE - FLOM - DANELAND! "
- "So, you have been to Babylon then."

Even when I catch him blatantly lying, he carries on the charade, seemingly oblivious to his own bullshit, it's actually quite impressive.

- "NoooooooOOOOOOoo - I - not - go - Babylon! - Bad - men - go – Babylon!
- "So, what happened? Tell me, did the ghosts take your boyfriend from "Daneland?""
- "It - true - It - True! - My - boyfriend - from - Daneland - he - go - in - sauna - I - not - see - heeem again - Ghost - take - him."

For a moment he looks genuinely forlorn, almost as if he actually gives a shit. Then he shoves another piece of fried pork in his mouth and carries on smiling. I'm so over trying to comfort him.

- " I suppose you're right, the prospect that he just fucked off with somebody else is completely implausible..."
- " Chai - Chai - Krap - He - go - in - dark - room - *SNIFF*- ghost - take - him - *SNIFF* - that - last - I - see – heeem. Now - I - have - new - boyfLiend - he - not - from - Daneland - he - from - Germanland - he - vely - rich - man - he - buy - me - ipad2 - he - not...."

It's at this point in every conversation with my secretary that I have to leave the building. Every day, without fail, he will piss all over my hopes for the future of our species. Seriously, somebody tell me how he functions? He's TWENTY. FUCKING. NINE!

Needless to say, all this talk of saunas had made me horny as fuck and luckily for me a weekend at Babylon is a guaranteed score.

A short taxi ride to Sathon, and suddenly all of my worries were behind me; I was cruising for physical intimacy, without any emotional complications, and luckily for me here in Bangkok, no questions are asked.

I'm not sure how it happened, was it the snatched glances? The surreptitious whistles as I walked past? As I strolled, smiling, through the dark rooms of Babylon, I noticed I was being hunted by a man. He was younger than me and very cute. I knew he was a top, Thai guys tend to make this distinction tediously obvious, and I knew he was hungry.

Like all good prey I made a show of aloofness, seemingly unaware of my fate.

Luckily the designers of Babylon are much more familiar with the rules of the hunt than "Le Trois Garcons." Perhaps, at heart, we're all old beasts who want to wear tiaras and get stuffed. However; there are no pretensions to eclectic design aesthetics in Babylon, it's clean and built for play, less sexy, sultry Lizard lounge, more filthy, easy clean Ikea. The man who was hunting me was skilled in the art, almost like he foresaw all of my twists and turns, and before I knew it, I was downstairs in a cubicle with his boyfriend. His boyfriend was Smiley and pretty and slender. They were both in their twenties with good bodies.

The hunter was horny, he removed his towel the second that he locked the door. His cock was thick and quite long, so he was probably used to local Thai queens complementing him. The three of us were naked in a cubicle peppered with glory-holes. The top pulled out condoms and lube, a little too eager perhaps, but too many men in their twenties need to feel the justification of physical penetration. The sophistication of mental stimulation eludes them. Perhaps they lack the subtleties of seduction? Or maybe he was just building up to his winning seduction line...

- "you suck me he finger you ass!"

To the point.

The thing with being locked in a dirty fuck cubicle with two horny Thai guys, is that you suddenly realize that 2 is company, but 3 is definitely allowed - they were so generous! There were so many possibilities here if, like me, you're not afraid of getting your hands dirty. The trouble with a top who has taken Viagra is that he can be too keen. He begins fucking me from behind while I suck the slender man.

The limited space means you can get supported in some really interesting positions. Use the 3 dimensions wisely, maybe utilise some of those ridiculous Bikram yoga positions you've been trying to forget.

Here's one of my favourite athletic moments:

BETTER BUMMING TIPS:

Start on the floor doggy style. Rim the slim guy and play with his balls, like your suckling a ripe peach.

Large top fucks you and as you relax and begin bucking back onto his cock, he turns on top of you, while he's still inside you. Your head should now be between his legs with his knees on the back of your shoulder blades. His cock is rock hard inside you, but bent down, away from his body. **Be warned** this probably isn't advisable if you happen to have a weak bladder or prostate problems, check with your GP just in case.

He puts his hands above his head on the floor either side of your feet. He pushes back onto his feet, which are wedged between the cubicle walls and the low ceiling. If you're doing it right, he should now resemble a sky diving accident.

Lift yourself up and support him by pushing your hands against the walls then push back onto his cock. You should feel his cock pressing forward. Easy does it.

Smiley, slender guy can slide in under you, and assume a position rather like a yoga "downward dog." If he's an experienced bottom he can slide backwards onto your cock.

You and the top really need to use your arms to steady everyone and get the rhythm right. You'll have to work it for a while to get the right pace - particularly if he's high or on Viagra.

Once you start getting into the swing of things; you, and the boys, are free to start exploring all the bell ends that appear in the glory holes.

It's truly a ridiculous sensation, but great fun. It's like being in a weird old fairground attraction. I kept expecting some greasy carny bloke to pop his head under the door and demand money. I'm beginning to find that sex IS ridiculous if you're doing it right; it should be fun and frivolous; laughed at and sweated over.

When I was younger, I had a tendency to attach some otherness to the intimacy, I would never really let go, I assumed that sex would be a meeting of heart and mind and body.

I was foolish to believe that, perhaps one day, I would meet these 3 faces in a monogamous coupling. Thinking about it, I assumed that all of this would be found in the arms of a significant other, someone who would be - dare I say it - *mine.* Well, love is for the young, but decadent threesomes are for lucky old queens. That's life.

Needless to say; after I had recounted my rather colourful anecdote to Alex, the Russian, I distinctly remember witnessing his jaw drop. He said:

- " You probably need to find some balance in your life."

I'm not entirely sure that he had heard me correctly, does he realise just how much balance it takes to spend an evening with a horny speed-freak and his boyfriend engaged in the most ludicrous contortionist sex?

I could see that Alex was a little disturbed by my revelation, I also had the sneaking suspicion that he was pissed off because I was not in awe of his, *oh so political,* relationship. Seriously, if the gay gods had wanted us to get married then they wouldn't have given us decadent fuck-pits and glory holes.

Fucking poseur!

As you can imagine the tension in his 3 way relationship was just insane. I had unwittingly become entangled in this Bermuda triangle of domestic lunacy and it was horrific.

There followed a high energy 30 minutes of shouting in Russian, leavings and retributions. It was all high drama. One of his boyfriends was jealous of him speaking to me, so he stormed off back to their hotel room. Shortly after, the other one left to talk with him so of course Alex felt left out *yada yada yada* then, with gracious apologies, they left me dancing alone. I never did get to ask them why so many Russians are into human trafficking these days, or why so many Russian whores OD in Pattaya, I guess I'll never know.

Perhaps he was shocked by my frankness. I could see he thought that I was belittling their relationship. That was not my intention. I have my threesome too! Three is a magic number. I have my friend in London who is rational, bordering on OCD, and I have my secretary here in Bangkok who thinks that the BTS runs on *"magic - fire - light."* If I need sex, then I can cruise my way through dark rooms and fuck a random.

Does that sound like a life lacking in balance to you?

Thinking about it, perhaps I shouldn't have equated my afternoon in a filthy fuck-hole, sliding around with two athletic studs, to his pretentious love life. Oh Well... Horses for courses as we say in England, horses for courses.

. . . . . . . . . . . . . . . .

## FUCKIN NOODLE SOUP!

If you're a blatant paedophile living in Thailand, your career options are limited to either being a children's entertainer, or "*teaching English*," in a Thai national school. Seriously, you should see some of the old perverts drunkenly wobbling off to school everyday, sweating and leering over schoolboys. It reminds me of the 70's in England. I remember all too well the "friendly" old men who would give me a bunk-up over the lowest of fences. Heady days of Werther's originals and Hovis bread. It was a childhood scripted by Alan Bennett, and shot with a sepia tint. In Thailand, the life of the poor is scripted in LA, and shot with a brash, neon glare. It's a harsh world imagined, if not instigated, by Terry Richardson. If you're lucky, you hook up with a fat, old *ferrang* drunk, who dresses as a clown and plays with children in a shopping mall.

The problem with packing all the paedos off to Thailand to, "*teach English,*" is that now we have to endure hearing what Thai people think. The majority of which is not worth listening to; it's generally something about "som tam," "sleeping," or "playing Facebook."

Take my secretary for instance (please, just take him), he doesn't stop talking. He talks so much it has become the background cacophony of my daily life. A piercingly staccato, camp monologue about his family, boyfriends (Giks), food, and Lady-FUCKING-Gaga! He doesn't even pause for breath, it's incredible:

- "He - say - he - my - boyfriend - why - I - not - go - to - Silom - wit - heem - I - say - cannot - he say - I - have - many - many - Giks - not - good -not - good - I say - he - not - love - me - he - look - at - other - boys - he - butterfly - he - say - he - not - butterfly - I – butterfly..."

At first, out of politeness, I would occasionally feign concern or even comprehension:

- "I think you should talk to him about it, let him know how you feel."

Now, I don't respond at all, he hasn't appeared to notice; he happily carries on all day, every day.

I can see why so many of the "*English teachers*" in Thailand, who aren't paedos, have become raging alcoholics. Being subjected to this incessant monotone all day is enough to drive anyone to drink. I like to think of Bangkok as the mausoleum of the 90's. If you're western, you should come here and drown in your own self absorbed excess. Drink it all, take it all, and fuck it all; just keep spending your money, and don't ever question the logic. Bangkok is the living end of post-modern nihilism. You are tolerated because you keep spending. The xenophobic Thai politic exclude every other lifestyle option to you, you are expected to be a total fuck-up.

The good thing about the passive aggressive Thai class system, is that anyone who doesn't fit the desired aesthetic - i.e. Asian, white skinned, fake European plastic nose - is considered, *"low,"* and therefore unattractive. This means you can have great fun fucking genuinely beautiful Thai people, who are considered to be ugly by their own people. Basically, they're much more fun and dirty when it comes to getting a decent fuck on.

Just thinking about smooth, dark skin stretched over strong bodies makes me hard...

So, the other day I was in the office...

- "... He - say - I - have - too- many - gik - I - NOT - BUTTERFLY - I - NOT - MESS - HEEM - AROUND - I - good - person - fLiens - tell - me - I - vely - honest - person - people - say - I - more - like - Brit - than - Thai..."

Suddenly he stopped talking... Shit. If only I had payed a modicum of attention, I might know the correct response. I broke out the emergency automatic reflex response:

- " Hmmm Yes. I think you should talk to him about it. Let him know how you feel."
- "... ChAAaaaaaAAAAaaaAi. Mister - you - vely - good - advice...."

I seized the opportunity to make my escape for an early lunch. I had a problem. In order to block out my idiot secretary, I had focused on thoughts of beautiful brown skinned men; so, I was ludicrously and inappropriately horny.

Luckily it's Bangkok, there are always options. For example:

1. Find a cute motorbike taxi driver and pay him 5oo baht for a fuck.

2.Go to the local massage parlour and pay the guy 500 baht tip for an oily wank.

3.Go to my local sauna, however it doesn't open until 6pm.

4.Go to the temple and get felt up by the monks again.

Unfortunately, desperation had clouded my judgement, I panicked! It suddenly occurred to me just how ridiculous this city is, I actually had viable options for a pre-lunch wank. At what point in my life had that become acceptable? I regained my composure and decided to go to my local noodle shop for lunch. Maybe I could drown my erection in delicious noodle soup.

Wrong.

The chap that works there has an incredibly sexy body. He is slender and well defined, with gorgeous dark chocolate skin. The Thai kids from the local school call him an *"Indian."* Like that's an insult. Who cares what they think, they're being taught by a fat, ignorant paedophille from Derby.

Noodle shop man always smiles at me and he flirts. Well, I say *"he flirts,"* it's actually a bit more obvious than that, he generally greets me with:

- "You have very beautiful face... I like to fuck you."

You know... Subtle. I had not planned this, but it suddenly occurred to me that I had taken an early lunch, and I was sitting in an empty noodle shop looking at a handsome, smiling, horny young man. I was hard. He asked me if I would like a massage and he pointed to a doorway behind the counter. When in Rome I thought to myself... He led me into a small multifunctional room that was shrine, utility room, storeroom, lounge, and bedroom. He proudly motioned to the faded yellow picture of the royal family on the wall, and insisted that I wai them. I'm not 100% sure on wai etiquette; however, I'm pretty sure I was supposed to give a high wai and a deep bow. Who knows? Who cares? I gave his small statue of the Buddah a wai; he smiled, is this what is means to pay *homage?*

He dropped his shorts and revealed a smooth, slender, long erection. It reminded me of a rather expensive cigar I had once smoked at the Cobden club in London. He kept on his apron, merely hoisting it to one side, and with a lazy wank motion he slid on a condom.

*BETTER BUMMING TIPS:*

There are none... You're basically getting fucked by a peasant in the back of his shop because your secretary is a whining cunt.

My face was wedged up against the picture of the royal family, and my trousers were around my ankles. I was crouched forward with my hands flat against the wall, he was hanging on to my hips and fucking me from behind like his life depended on it. Could this get any classier? Oh yes it could! I looked down between my legs, and I noticed that he still had on his grimy pair of lime green Crocs. You know, the ones comically designed to look like animal feet? Brilliant. His legs were spread wide in order to give his frantic thrusts more traction. It was one of the most liberating experiences of my life. I had an epiphany, who the fuck cares!

He came quickly and graciously furnished me with the desired reach around, so everyone was happy.

After he pulled up his shorts and adjusted his apron; he washed his hands, preyed to the Buddha, and went back to cooking my noodle soup.

It's great to know that you've been fucked by a penitent man who has good standards of personal hygiene. For the briefest of moments, I felt completely ashamed of myself. Then it dawned on me, who really cares? Noodle-shop man doesn't care. Why should anyone care? It's like it never happened. Everyday I continue to ignore my idiot secretary, and I pop out for noodle soup made by a man who calls me beautiful. I'm not sure I'll ever fuck the fast food man ever again, but it was an experience.

Oddly enough I can no longer stomach the taste of MSG, or the sight of lime green Crocs.

# PART 9 – THONG LOR – APRIL – 2011

## FUCKING LIARS!

Many people who are new to Thailand might be confused by the concept of, "saving face." Apparently, it's a cultural tradition that is supposed to signify politeness. In my opinion, western people might confuse it with the concept of, *"lying,"* because it is!

Forget all that guidebook horse-shit telling you to, "*respect this quaint local tradition.*" It's basically about deceiving people, and then not feeling bad about it. It does take a bit of getting used to.

I love it.

Don't believe me? Try working here. I have a secretary that is camper than me, and I'm wearing a pink shirt and a fedora. Next to him, I'm John Wayne. Don't get me wrong, He's brilliant and lovely, it's just that he's completely useless. In order to stop myself having a meltdown every-time I look at his smiling, lying face; I simply ignore everything he says. We get along much better this way. So essentially, he spends his time Skyping his boyfriend(s) in Germany, and I run a department on my own. Trust me, it saves time and energy.

A typical conversation with him goes something like this:

- "Have you sent those e-mails I asked you to send yesterday?"
- "Yes, yes, ChaAaaaaaAaaaAaaaaiiii Kaaap."
- "It's very important. Have you sent them?"
- "ChhhHhhhai Kaaap, I - send - them – yesterday – krap - don't worry – mister - I send them yesterday... Krap."
- " I don't mind if you haven't. Please, just tell me the truth, have you sent them or not? If you haven't I can send them today."
- "Yes - Yes - I – not – lie – I - tell – you - truth. I - send - them – yesterday."

Of course he hasn't sent them!

Of course I can't fire him because he comes with the job!

Of course I'm completely jealous!

If only everyone in life could be so utterly useless.

AAAAAARRRRGH!

So, when someone calling himself, *"Rimtong123,"* on a gay shag-site, sends me a message saying he can fuck me all night and it will be the best fuck of my life - forgive me for being a little skeptical.

His profile stated that he was 29, looking for friends, single, muscular and Asian, not into drugs, strictly top, not into fisting or, "*dirty*," oh yeah, and he likes art. HAHAHAHHAHAH.

A cultured bummer from Bangkok, *who knew?* He sounds just like the type of boy you could boast about to your Nan

I was new to the whole gay web dating thing, so I thought, *why not?*

Long story short, I end up at his flat in Sathon soi 1. His real name is "Wut," well, that's what he said. Within in a few moments he had contradicted himself 3 times. It was all bullshit. I was hoping it was a language barrier thing, but it wasn't, he was totally full of shit. He showed me his "art;" well, what can I say? We live in a world where Damien Hirst paints really shitty parrots, so why not call this guy's *tissue paper on a canvas* art? To be honest, I would have been more impressed if he had just shown me a huge text book cock'n'balls, with dribbles of spunk and hair on the bollocks. In fact it probably would have been more authentic and visceral. Who cares about his art? It reeked of crystal meth and unfulfilled ambition. It's the kind of thing suburban people might put in their toilets in order to match the fittings. Anyway, this guy was cheeky as fuck and he had, "amazing shag," written all over him.

Maybe that's what his Buddhist tattoos were all about? Are they some sort of mystical marker for dirty fucks? He told me that his tattoos were, "for good fortune, good luck, they make rich!" Apparently, a monk had tattooed him, so he was *blessed.* Strange; it only seems to be poor meth heads, without any hope of moving up in the Thai world, that appear to be *blessed.*

I'm not one to cast aspersions, but doesn't that suggest that, maybe, the tattoos don't work? I mean, you don't see wealthy, *Hi-So* Thai people wandering around covered in religious tattoos do you? If they have tattoos, they are rock and roll tattoos, and they help to reiterate the fact that they will never have to do a days work in their lives.

Anyway, he had a rocking body, tight and toned, and a massively cheeky smile that screamed, "DEVIANT!" I hate to be a clichéd old queen, but what can I say? Naughty boys do it for me. This guy was naughty.

I noticed he kept on his talisman pendants - I love the look of those clumsy, amber and ivory things knocking against his supple, brown skin.

He took control by calling me "baby." I'm bigger and older than him, but it was flattering, and it didn't sound quite as ridiculous as it looks when I type it here. Without agreement, he had cast our roles for the night, and I was his "baby."

I've never been anyone's, "baby," before.

It's so fifties.

I felt like I should be worrying about getting knocked up by the guy who owns the holiday camp. Whatever it is, for me, he's got it. I just let him do his thing... He... Fucking... LOVES... IT!

It was blatantly obvious that Rimtong123 had been smoking crystal. He wasn't crazy high, but he was, "up." Hence the fact that he kept getting "*confused*," with his stories.

I don't think we'll be needing the services of Sherlock Holmes, or even Nancy Drew, to figure out the mystery of Rimtong123, but for the sake of a good story, let's look at the evidence:

1. He told me he didn't do drugs. Then he told me he did do drugs - sometimes - and that he had smoked a little pipe earlier - but he wasn't high.
2. He told me he had been single for a long time. Then he told me had just broken up with his partner from Italy. Later, he told me that he was in an open relationship with a man from the Netherlands. Finally, he informed me he was off to visit his boyfriend in Switzerland at the end of the month.
3. During our session he answered the land line several times, and spoke in English to a few Europeans. I really didn't know who they were, and I don't want to know, but they were clearly unaware of each others existence. He didn't seem to care about the fact that I was English, and could understand every word that he was saying. He told them all he was sick and had decided not to go out with his friends, he was having an early night in on his own.

I AM IN THE ROOM! I CAN HEAR YOU!

Brilliant!

I know I should be saying something about how bad he was etc, etc, etc, etc, but I can't. As an artist, I have the utmost respect for anyone that can spin a complicated yarn, especially one with as many plot lines as the Rimtong123/ Painting123/ Wut narrative. It's probably the most enduring piece of original artwork that the man will ever accomplish. It beats the shit out of putting tissue paper on a canvas.

I really didn't care what he did. I was just in it for the shag. As for the Europeans he was robbing, do they really need me telling them that he's stringing them along? I had no intention of seeing him again after that night, so he was their problem, not mine.

I left as the morning sun lit up the faded yellow of his curtains. For a short while, the madness of Bangkok seemed to make some sense. We arranged to meet later that day, but it was an empty promise. I lied. I knew I would need sleep, and I knew he would be getting high and fucking someone else.

Even though I lied just to get out of his bed. I wasn't messing him about. I told him several times that I wouldn't see him again, not to play hard to get, I meant every word. As is always the way, nothing turns a naughty man on more than being told, "NO." So, from the next day, he started the phone calls, the messages, the texts... "Baby please, I want fuck you again..." It was tragic.

I would be lying if I said that I didn't think about saying yes. Seriously, when you are single, thirty something and someone is pestering you everyday for great sex, you can't help but get a semi on. I haven't said yes. Maybe we all play out our little deceptions. Perhaps that's what turned me on to him so much, his blatant honesty about lying. Whatever he's doing, it's clearly working out for him. He may have been a complete fantasist, but he told the truth about one thing, he did fuck me all night, and it was pretty much one of the best fucks I've ever had.

. . . . . . . . . . . . . .

FUCKING IDIOTS!

- Me – "You look good. You have a great body."
- Beautiful man - "Yeah I know, like, I'm, like, a model. I model shit…"
- Me – "So… You're a shit model? Cool, How's that working out for you?"
- Beautiful man - "It, like, totally sucks, like, some shit is like, sooooo shit to model."
- Me – "I'm genuinely fascinated, tell me more! How did you get into modeling shit? Where do you model shit? What sort of shit do you model?"
- Beautiful man – "Oh…You know, Like clothes and shit… I got into it because I was, like, bored and like, my friend had some new shit she needed modeling on the catwalk for, like, her show

in, like, London. Like, London UK right? So I, like, said I'd do it, like, "what the fuck!" Right? You know? I don't know, you know? Like, I don't know… All sorts of shit, like, whatever…"

It's conversations like these that are the reason why sex tourism in Thailand is so prolific. Surely nobody sets out to become a sex obsessed walking libido? We're driven to it! How else are you supposed to stop this man from talking, other than by asking him to fuck you? Believe me, this wasn't a language barrier thing. The guy's a moron. He's a lovely moron, a handsome moron, but a moron nonetheless.

I've read this back and think I sound like a cock. Let me make this clear. I know that not all beautiful people are idiots. I also know that clever people can be cunts. But seriously, this guy is supposed to be a qualified civil engineer. He has a master's degree from the best university in the country. He constructs buildings, "and shit…" Hence, the buildings in Bangkok NOT built by European firms start falling down after 6 months.

I'm not suggesting everyone in Bangkok should be Steven Hawking, but sometimes, just sometimes, I would love a conversation here with a beautiful person that is more, "*MENSA*," than, "*MENCAP*."

His apartment is huge. However, I had trouble fitting into his en-suite bedroom on account of his massive ego. What on earth was I thinking? In a strange way, I was reminded of myself when I was in my late twenties. I was thinking that maybe, behind the narcissistic facade, there was a clever guy that would get it… My bad… A vanity shag is never a good thing. This was doomed from the start.

In my defense, he had a good body, really toned, and a typical Thai celebrity face, complete with the huge, ridiculous fake nose lift. So, really, what's a single gay to do? You're in Bangkok – THE CLUE IS IN THE NAME!

I'm into anonymous fucking. But if it's a one on one sex date at a guys flat, surely it's good manners to acknowledge that there is somebody else in the room? No? Okay, maybe I am being a selfish old drama queen – it's all about ME!

He fucked like he was inspired by Hitler.

He told me how good he was at fucking me - while he was fucking me. Naturally, he liked being on top, pounding away with his eyes closed like he was conquering a third world country... NOT good.

I had enough of being banged like I was a teenager at a Slipknot concert, so I pushed him back and I straddled him.

BETTER BUMMING TIP:

Lie the man on his back with a cushion under the arch of his back – Asian men love their little comforts – straddle him, then push back and down with your hands so you slide down the tops of his thighs. His cock should be inside you pressing forward onto your pelvis – I'm guessing that's where your prostate should be – however; I'm not a doctor, maybe you can check this with your GP? Next, begin contracting your abs, pull in and back, as though someone has a string around your midriff, and is tugging you backwards. Flex your pelvic floor muscles, in men, they are the muscles that connect the pubic bone to your tailbone, rather like a hammock (in keeping with the whole Asian theme). You should be rocking your pelvis forward, like you're doing a stomach crunch. If you perform this motion quite quickly, you will be hardly moving, but you'll both be loving it. I like to lean down and bite his lower ear-lobes. It's good to get quite vocal at this point…

This guy was really letting out the vocals.

Anyway, I caught his attention for the briefest of moments, his expression was one of wonder. He was like a child who had suddenly come to terms with the fact that he wasn't the centre of the universe anymore; there were, in fact, other people in the world. He looked deep into my eyes with a look of complete bewilderment. Perhaps that was his Botox?

His Blackberry vibrated and he began instant messaging, while he was still inside me. That was my cue to leave. I got dressed and he said nothing, he just lay there looking at me. He asked for my number, I gave him the number of X men delivery service, the worst dial-a-ride service in Bangkok.

So what did I learn from this? Well, I'm not sure, maybe I'm not cut out for fucking the Thai 'Hi-So' men in Thong Lor, Perhaps I should stick to fucking motorbike taxi drivers. Maybe I should just stick to people my own age? Or maybe I should sleep with people I can actually talk to?

I'm a total fucking idiot.

I have since seen his face plastered on a billboard on the way to the airport. He has a look of total amazement and wonder, it's exactly the same as his come face. I'm guessing it's his look, his own personal, "blue steel?"

# PART 8 - KHAO SAN - MARCH – 2011

I have lost count of the number of drunken rants I had in London at ridiculous times in the morning over the meaning of words. In the end people gave up listening, but that didn't change the fact that I was right. 'Rodent' for example: Why would being called a rodent be considered an insult? However much it infuriates me to this very day, the word 'rodent' is undeniably loaded with negative connotations. Just allow the word to roll around your thoughts and you will be inundated with foul images of desperate scavenging mammals. Rodents exist in a disease ridden, hideous part of our imagination; a place that has forgotten that squirrels are essentially rats with fluffier tails.

So when I say "Kim Soon reminded me of a rodent," try to conjure up fluffy images of timid creatures; because there really is no other word to best describe Kim Soon.

Kim Soon reminded me of a rodent. Even for a 12 year old Thai boy he was tiny. His head was filled with sleek black eyes the colour of pathos. He sat at the front of my class and eyed me with pursed serenity. At first I assumed that he was bullied by the other more boisterous members of the class; not necessarily in a violent way - he's far too sweet to have to endure that - but in a psychological manner which is often more cruel. Looking back, having taught at the English summer-school for two weeks, I think that Kim Soon preferred his own company and found the endless jokes about bum-holes rather boring. I am inclined to agree, even the most amusing fart joke can wear a little thin after a class of teenage boys has dragged it out for nearly 2 hours.

Little Kim Soon.

He occasionally removed his glasses and meticulously rubbed them like a squirrel buffing up a particularly tasty seed. He was immaculately presented and his lilac *'Milka cow'* pencil case was clean and perfectly organized. He completed all of the written work for the class in approximately 2 minutes and then, more often than not, he had a tendency to curl up and snooze like a dormouse with his little arms curled neatly under his head.

I hadn't the heart to wake him most days, his work was always above standard - plus - if he could sleep through the pandemonium of an M2 English class, then I would have little hope of shaking him from his slumber.

It was my last full day teaching at the school IEP (Intensive English Program). There had been an hour of torrential rain and the grounds were flooded. It was unbearably hot due to the fact that the air-conditioning could not be used when it rained, as the boys informed me, "it will big bang!" It was imperative that I prepare the boys for the end of program test, which was proving difficult. I was beginning to understand why many of the teachers cheated in order to save their jobs.

Such is the education system in Thailand.

If the pupils fail then the teacher is held accountable.

On that particular day I felt the need to wake Kim Soon and check that he was adequately prepared for the test. Also, I had brought prizes of sweets and DVD's for the students who had performed best throughout the course. His written work was exceptionally good, therefore I had decided to award him a small packet of Ferrero rocher. I approached his desk and gently called his name.

He rubbed his eyes behind his glasses and then peered up at me with a look that could have been animated by Walt-Disney.

"Kim Soon. Is everything alright at home? Are you getting enough sleep?"

He looked somewhat bemused, a look which I had mistakenly assumed to be one of concentrated translation. It was in fact a look of bafflement at the ridiculousness of my question.

- "I was awake last night watching live news reports from Libya on the BBC. England is bombing all those people. I think it sad. Between that and the disaster in Japan I don't want to live in this world. What is the point of learning English if we are going to die?"

Coming from a poor English background I am used to disillusion. It is our inheritance, our birthright. We are a people raised on a strict diet of miserable resignation to our nations former glory, but to hear such words coming from one so sweet – well, I must admit I was horrified. What have we done as a race to inspire such disenchantment in our children?

"The English language has given us many beautiful things Kuhn Kim soon. Watching too much television will only depress you; believe me, it has become an industry based on exploiting misery."

He squinted his large oval eyes and then subjected me to a gaze that instantly reminded me of Bambi. However, it was a post-modern Bambi. A Bambi that was cynically aware from the opening credits that his Mother was to be shot and the whole *life* thing was just about killing time.

- "It's the language for murders and killers."

"Then try not to murder the language of killers Kuhn Kim Soon! I assume you mean, "it's the language of killers and murderers." Although I rather like the idea of it being the 'language for murders,' it's very Agatha Christie."

"Sorry. English is the language of murdelers."

"That's better, try to remember the 'r' sound is different to the 'l' sound so it's 'r, R, Rrrrrr, muRRRRderers' different to 'L L L Language'."

"MuRRRRRRRRderers."

"Correct."

He mouths the word 'murderers' several times in silence which I found weirdly unsettling.

- "Why is there so much anger? What is the point of living in this world?"
- "There is so much to live for Mr Kim Soon, you wait and see..."

He looked at me and I swear there was disbelief behind his glasses. To a degree, I must agree with his rather bleak view; I say 'to a degree.' I happen to like The Smiths, but an entire hour in the company of Morrisey and his prepubescent whining would drive me mad. I say 'hour,' it would probably be about five minutes before I would have to scream:

"CHEER UP YOU MISERABLE OLD TWAT! YOU DON'T LIVE IN MANCHESTER ANYMORE! IT'S NOT RAINING AND YOU HAVE A JOB!"

I decide to change the subject.

- "Are you prepared for your test? Is there anything that you need to ask me?"
- "Yes. Do you think the aliens come and save us? I like to meet them, everyone tell me they are friendly and intelligent. Will they save us from the English speaker?"
- "That would be, 'English speakers' Kim Soon, it's plural because there is more than one English speaker. You've done Well Kuhn Kim soon, you have worked hard, you have won a prize for your written work."

He gave a flash of a smile and for a moment I regretted the need to rely on bribery, a shameless diversionary tactic on my part; anything to stop the sound of disillusion ringing in my ears. It was a sound not unfamiliar to me once upon a time...

. . . . . . . . . . . . . .

According to many theorists and cultural commentators the rave scene was a direct result of a “disillusioned youth.”

I disagree.

Firstly, anyone who uses the term ‘cultural commentator’ needs to stop reading Camille Paglia and get a real job.

Secondly, as far as I’m concerned the rave scene was a lot of excitable teenagers getting high in a warehouse. Having fun in a field comes naturally to English people, it’s what we do best.

Believe it or not, there was a time when dance music was quite eclectic and exciting. It was all loosely arranged into vague sub genres; such as hardcore, acid house, house, techno, but all of that seemed quite irrelevant. On the night, a Dj would play any track needed to set the rush in motion. It was about invention, inspiration and - dare I say it - fun.

Are those halcyon days the product of a rose tinted imagination?

As with any popular movement or scene, the elements are quickly commodified and replicated and packaged. Before you know it, it’s not fun anymore, it’s “cool.”

One minute it’s all glow-stick lunacy, driving around under the influence of mind-bending psychedelics in a car full of gurning squaddies. The next thing you know, you’re at some slick club having a conversation with a particularly smug prick who says something along the lines of:

“Yeah... He’s all gone a bit hand-baggy for me, I remember seeing him back in 89 and he was the nuts. He’s gone way too commercial...”

It’s generally men that are to blame for this idiocy. An awful lot of men have a phenomenal capacity to suck the fun out of everything and then bemoan the fact that it’s boring. All of a sudden you have a room full of bedroom DJ’s harping on about being, *“credible,”* and dull promoters putting together programs consisting of hours and hours of the same monotonous sounds. It becomes all about fractured sub-groups and compartmentalized tribes. It's business and money and paraphernalia, what's forgotten is the simple fact that having fun in a warehouse was the objective of the whole exercise.

I often wonder what has become of the libertine. So many of us were sold on a hedonistic life of dancing without consequence; what happens when the living-fast and the dying-young doesn't happen? Living without consequences has consequences.

It's an all too familiar tale.

Your job doesn't actually pay enough for you to own your own home or pay off your student debts, so you rely on overdrafts. Your life is now owed to your bank. You crash headlong into middle age and suddenly the music isn't working for you anymore, it's a sham, you don't know what to believe. Next thing you know, you're one of those miserable old drunks that you swore you would never become.

You have to laugh...

Khao San road reminds me of Camden in many respects. It's full of people still chasing a dream that's over. I know. For a while I was that man.

I remember sitting in Camden last year with another 30 something rocker/raver. He was bitching and moaning about shit contemporary music. Basically I don't think anyone was interested in what he was doing.

- "It's all been done before and better! I remember seeing Oasis; pissed all over that Frans fuckin' Ferdinand and all that shite. They can't play their fuckin' instruments. I know fuckin' music, played it for fuckin' years, you want to get a bit of the Verve going on; you know, fuckin' proper music!"

Needless to say he was a boring cunt.

Old rockers and ravers tend to occupy a space that is neither visceral nor real. It's a space that is beyond time and age. They are both noble and pathetic.

I have drunk myself stupid here in Khao San road.

It's a really strange place.

It's not like anywhere else in Bangkok. Some people love it and some people hate it. For me it remains the only place in the world where I have nearly been run over by a barbecue... I say barbecue, it was an old woman driving a bike full of glaring charcoal and meat.

I love it's oddness and eccentricity. It is everything that Camden wishes it could be; but can't be, because of odd things like *the law*. It's the perfect place to indulge all of your disillusions, and delusions. It's full of greying hippies who are still learning to juggle, a weird hall of mirrors reflecting everything and nothing. It exudes pretension even though it is full of people who are trying their very hardest not to be pretentious.

It's funny, even though the place is full of tourists, you never actually meet any tourists. People are usually *'travellers'* or *'on a stop-over'* it's almost as if the word 'tourist' has become a dirty word, like rodent. A tourist is someone who goes to Spain and demands a fried breakfast. Here *'travellers'* live on Pad-Thai and spring-rolls and buckets of mad Thai whiskey. They live on the illusion that they are something more than tourists.

I remember I had drunk too much whiskey.

I was talking to a man my age but he looked older. Apparently he knew everything and had been everywhere. He looked like he was the sort of man who had lost-it at a *'Levellers'* gig in the early nineties, and never really got it back.

I am of the opinion that white people should never have dreadlocks past the age of 30. I don't know why, it just seems all wrong. Long hair? Sure why not! Long unwashed hair with bits stuck in it? NO! It smacks of something that Tim Westwood would have done if he had remained at the vicarage and not discovered gangsta rap.

I had met Teemo outside a bar on the street and we were drinking, he was pleasant enough company; although, where Teemo was from remains a mystery. The accent said Essex, but the dreadlocks said home-counties.

I made the mistake of telling him that I used to go to raves all over England. As is the way with rave talk, all he did for the next hour was tell me about all the parties and drugs he had "done."

- "Back in 92 at Raindance we were all double dropping them doves, we was off our fuckin' heads."
- "Yeah, the first batch of Mitsubishi's were rockin but then they started getting cut with smack - sledgy as fuck!"
- "Remember the pink New Yorkers back in 89? Blew me away man, they don't make 'em like that anymore..."

I decided to step in and let him know I knew the score, even though I looked like a dusty old teacher.

- "No way Teemo, I had those New Yorkers and went to see *Guru Josh* and *Adamski* one night..."

For some reason I blush, and it's clear that I sound exactly like a pissed up aunt at a shit wedding. I mean really, who cares anymore right? His expression assumed a look of awe.

- "*Guru Josh* in 89. On New yorkers man. WOW."

He seems agitated and continually shakes his head in a manner reminiscent of a sham Indian shaman. It was clear that I had elicited from him something akin to reverential simpatico.

- "No way. I'm going to see the guru josh project next month - doing all the re-mixes, yeah, infinity 2011! No fucking way.

Would have loved to have seen him back in 89 though man."

Naturally, as with most ravers, 1989 was Teemo's halcyon year, nothing will ever match up to the drugs or the parties.

Was it really?

Am I capable of being objective about all of this?

It was fun, true, it was exciting and new; we were all young, it was our time to shine. I had just left school, and it was my summer of love. I was running free, scurrying around the country, parties and rock and roll. The halcyon sunrise dances occurred many seasons later throughout the 90's, but who can ever be sure of exact dates?

Let's face it - we were loaded.

It suddenly occurred to me that Teemo had been living in 1989 for many years. In fact he was still there now, except it wasn't the real 1989. It wasn't the wars and the dismal politics of Thatcher and Bush. It wasn't the fall of the Russian empire and the Berlin wall. None of that for him; for Teemo, all those free parties had blended into one long festival. It had come to define him, as it had defined me for a while. I chose to stop living in the past, but a part of me is slightly jealous...

Mostly I just wanted to wash his hair.

Not in a gay way, but as an act of human kindness.

- "The best music in the world was made back then." He says nodding sagely.

Then the unthinkable happened. Teemo looked at me bemused and baffled, he could not quite believe what I was saying I uttered the unutterable. I broke the golden rule.

- "Yeah I know what you mean. The Stone Roses made some of my favourite records ever, EVER; I mean Sally Cinnamon is perfect pop, but whenever I saw them live they were totally shit. They just couldn't play at all, they were awful."

He shook his head again; not in the manner of a fraudulent Asian spiritual leader, but this time in disgust. He ran his hands the length of his dreads and then reached for his tobacco tin (silver, lovingly embossed with a naff picture of the Buddha).

- "you saw the Roses? You saw the Roses and thought they were shit?"
- "Well yes... I saw them twice. They were rubbish. I loved the records, but live, they were terrible, out of time, out of tune, if it hadn't been for Reni on the drums..."

He looked like a fish that had just been bludgeoned.

- "Bullshit. You've never seen the Roses man. Really? No way man. I bet they were fucking mental!"

I suddenly remembered that I had become one of those men at parties that had sucked the fun out of everything. It was to be expected really. These days I'm a stuffy old teacher. My life has become a never ending plethora of lesson plans and confusing grammatical conventions. I had enjoyed the gigs because I was a teenager excitedly seeking out the next after party adventure. I preferred watching Aerosmith at Donington to The Stone Roses. Steve Tyler in a spandex jumpsuit doing back-flips, now that's rock and roll. In my mind The Stone Roses had been a bit miserable, but for the sake of the myth; the legend, and for ridding Teemo's face of that weird expression - I decided the grown up thing to do was lie.

- "Yeah, the gigs were amazing, they were the best band ever."

On Khao San rd it's easy to understand how myths rise from nothing and suddenly become irrefutable facts. It is one small road in Bangkok, nothing appealing about it, nothing special about it. There is nothing even typically 'Thai' about it. It has more foreigners than any other part of Bangkok. It has some of the shittest accommodation in Bangkok. Having no public transport links, it is quite out of the way and it's really awkward to find. It has the most expensive and ripest prostitutes in Bangkok. It has some of the worst night clubs in Bangkok and some of the most expensive street food in Bangkok. However, for whatever reason, everything about Bangkok for so many people is to be found within that street...

The name alone conjures up decadent anarchy.

KHAO SAN.

*LEGENDARY KHAO SAN.*

Just allow the word to roll around your thoughts and you will be inundated with images of drunken debauchery, beautiful people and beautiful food, dancing until the daylight.

So people come in their millions to experience this once in a life-time road of ill-repute. In doing so they actually make it happen, it actually lives up to the hype. It embodies all the counter-cultural expectations of anarchy and fun.

. . . . . . . . . . . . . .

Several days before the IEP at the school, it had been brought to my attention that I had to renew my visa. My school administration were terrible at sorting this out. So I made my way to Chaeng Wattana immigration office situated seemingly in the middle of nowhere, several miles from the end of the BTS line. It's an easy trip, a marvelous building, just quite an odd place. It's all very swish and contemporary; however, the presence of Thai women shuffling around the huge modern space in slippers munching on deep fried pork-knuckle, gives it a down-at-home Thai feel.

The first thing I noticed upon arriving at the Enormous new government building, was just how many of the immigration security staff drive brand new BMW or Mercedes cars. Perhaps the reason I had noticed this seemingly random piece of information had something to do with my being there in the first place.

I had been stopped and asked for my papers by the police on my way to work at a school. Apparently I had missed my 90 day registration. Nobody at the school had told me that this was a condition of my employment. I didn't know this of course, as far as I was concerned my permit was still valid; but no, I was working illegally. Just trying to negotiate this whole work permit situation with Thai schools has been really awkward. The administration will frequently give misinformation which means you end up submitting endless photo-copies and forms and still ending up without any legitimacy. After many uncomfortable seconds the policeman said that if I paid the, "fine," of 2000 baht it would be "easy." Strangely enough I gave him the 2000 and he wondered off without even taking my details.

To those of you who are unfamiliar with the rate of exchange here in Thailand, I have composed a small list which should be of some help.

2000 baht = £40

Apparently, this amounts to a, "fine," for illegally working without a valid permit.

This also gets you an hour with the most beautiful whore in the room at a soapy massage emporium.

By comparison, this is also the average weekly wage of many Thai workers - although most unskilled workers earn much, much less.

So it seems a rather strange fact that many workers at the immigration office can afford brand new cars. Or is it? Could the whole economy here be oiled by bank loans and bribes? I dread to think.

Immigration offices are the same the world over, they are impersonal places that exist between worlds. They are places that reek of desperation and disillusion. Dreams are made and brutal truths are exorcised within these walls. I remember feeling rather sorry for everyone that queued here. Bureaucracy is a game played out for the amusement of people who are essentially quite bored, endless systems of form stamping and job creation.

I had been queuing for approximately 2 hours, when my number was finally called. The lovely Thai security lady came forward and announced they would all be stopping for lunch. Which they did. So I sauntered off to the staff cafe for a much needed bowl of noodle soup.

Unfortunately my queue friend decided to join me. We all love a good queue friend, it makes the whole queue experience more bearable. However, it's one thing to stand in a queue with a posh Englishman who has decided to spend months of his gap year as a Buddhist monk; it's quite another to enjoy noodle soup with him.

His robes looked rather shabby and unkempt. As a British monk he should have had the decency to look impeccable if he knew he was going to immigration. Looking at him I felt oddly patriotic as though he was letting the side down in some way by not washing his robes. I'm not entirely sure why that bothered me so much. His name was Josh.

I paid for his soup, monks don't carry any money apparently, (presumably he was carrying the 2000 needed to renew his visa?) and we sat at one of the staff tables. We smiled courteously at the security staff who were sitting adjacent. They seemed in good cheer. Probably laughing at the dirty western monk, something to tell the kids at Song Kran. His dirty robes really troubled me.

- "Cheers for the soup bro... Nice shirt, you working here at the moment?"

He avoided my gaze and my attempt to reply and carried on. Talking over me like I wasn't even there. I guess this was all part of his journey to find his inner Josh.

- "Yeah I mean Like, spirituality is something that's missing from England, right? We just don't get it, right?"

Another rhetorical question?

- "I mean we're all just so uptight about it. They totally get the whole spiritual thing here. It's amazing right? They're such a peaceful people, they have so much fun... Simple life and truth. It's like a totally chilled religion man, like totally chilled... Yeah, I'm probably going to do this for another couple of months and then go check out Vietnam or Cambodia; it's been a lot of work being a monk. I came here straight after uni too, so I really need a break..."

I can't remember exactly why I wanted to strangle him, but I do remember wrestling with my own inner zen in order to say something gracious.

- "I suppose if you are going to believe in a religion, you might as well believe in one that is truly peaceful and respects wisdom. What did you study at university?"

- "I did film studies at St Andrews; 2.2, not bad considering I was pissed the whole time; nearly missed my finals going to a rave in London. It was sooOooooOOOo funny."
- "I'm glad that worked out for you. Can I ask you what made you decide to become a monk?"

I forced myself to imagine the other pervy sex-tourists and Israeli bullies that had latched onto me during my travels; by comparison, Josh is rather sweet and harmless. Like me, he's quite insignificant and inconsequential. We're harmless eccentrics really.

- "Well, I've always loved Buddhist philosophy and I wanted to do something different with my gap year. I mean EVERYONE goes travelling these days, but I didn't want to like, "go travelling," I wanted to; you know, experience the real Thailand. So I ended up at this wicked temple in the north, it's beautiful, really peaceful, I decided to stay an extra month. You should check it out."

The more he talked, I couldn't help thinking he was a bit of a twat, which is pretty mean of me I know.

- "It sounds beautiful. I love the countryside. Thailand is beautiful, but my spirit - for all its sins - is here in Bangkok."

I remember getting turned on by his shaved head and grubby robe. I looked at him rather longingly for a second and wanted to run my fingers over his naive, stubbly bonce. I have no idea why. Maybe it's because he had a touch of the strawberry blond? Or perhaps it was because he was clearly a bit of an idiot? I don't know. Is it wrong to be turned on by a dim-witted posh boy in monk drag?

It was a fantasy, a fiction, it stopped me from hating him for 5 seconds.

I made a mental note to add orange robes to my dressing up box, which I kept under my bed for, um, *special occasions*. Personally, I preferred to experience *the real Thailand* through the medium of kinky man-drag. I happen to be one of the few ex-pats who can boast about the fact that I have collected almost every colour of motor bike taxi vest in existence. If that isn't your thing, at the drop of a hat I can become a soldier, sailor, nurse, security guard or pizza delivery man...

Following lunch we sauntered back into the space that resembled a departure lounge. The security guards had eaten everything in the canteen and were back almost on time, and so began the whole back and forward process of things not being stamped that should be stamped.

Whilst waiting for my final stamp I took a seat next to Josh. He had yet to see the initial stamp-lady, so goodness knows how long he was going to have to wait. It's hard to say exactly what was going on in that hollow head of his; however, he seemed quite chipper.

- "Yeah it's cool, I'm just hanging out waiting and shit... Total meditation zone."

I was beginning to warm to him.

- "So Josh what do you think of the real Thailand?"

I asked rather cheekily, I didn't mean to sound so acerbic, it just came naturally.

- "No way, this isn't like the REAL Thailand. This is like, just an office on the way to the real Thailand. It's all cool though, just wait until you experience the real Thailand..."

Just then my conversation with a thick English monk was interrupted by the arrival of a Russian whore.

As with *'rodent'* or *'tourist'* the term *'whore'* has become riddled with negative connotations; some of which can be seen as quite uncomplimentary. Just allow the word *'whore'* to roll around your thoughts. Your mind will be filled with rancid, disease ridden images, which neglect the fact that many sexual relationships come with a price. I must make it clear I don't mean *'whore'* in any particularly negative sense of the word. In fact, I applaud the ability to ask someone to give you money in exchange for sex; I wish I could be that confident or desirable. What I meant to say is that this woman was clearly a "*repulsive whore.*"

She was a whore with a capital "W"

She tottered in heavily pregnant, angrily balanced on the most uncomfortable heels and smoking a thin cigarette, which she dragged as though her baby's life depended on it. She was positively dripping with bad hair and cheap gold. Accompanying her was an interesting character, an extremely jolly Thai gentleman who wore a lovely grey suit and a mischievous smile. The odd thing about him was that he had only one buttock. Believe me, I am a man that notices such things, and I can say with all sincerity that I have never seen anything like it before. He lacked a left buttock.

He was a genuine limping mincer.

Having spent some time here in the land of smiles, I feel qualified to say that the pair screamed, "*PATTAYA!*"

For those of you who don't know, Pattaya is an absolutely rotten place, particularly if you happen to be a single gay male, it's the fag end of gay life, no good will ever come from there.

The whore had the look of somebody who was beautiful in her day, but now she was embittered and sour. She had clearly got knocked up and settled for a luxury condo in Pattaya, which had given her a sense of superiority. It was also clear by the way she ordered the limping mincer around that the father of her baby was someone significant. Anyone could see she would rather not be there, in all fairness, being heavily pregnant, who would?

I offered her my seat (English to the core) which she refused with a flap of her cigarette hand. The smoldering fag-end fell and gently landed in my lap, I swiftly knocked it to the floor and stubbed it with my shoe.

No damage.

She lit another cigarette and stood staring, wild eyed at me, like she was daring me to say something.

*"*Oh don't worry about it love;" I said with all sincerity, "I've had more flaming butts on this lap than you've had hot dinners!"

I'm not sure where that came from or why, she hesitated looking somewhat confused. Her eyes rolled back and fell upon her chuckling mono-bunned companion.

She began shouting at him in Russian, and to his credit, he never once stopped smiling. After he placated her with broken Russian, she strutted past me and found another seat further away, ironically just below the, *"No Smoking"* sign. She continued to stare at me icily through a haze of smoke. Turns out you can't please all of the whores all of the time. The cheery Thai fellow gathered her papers and then limped off behind the counter. In full view of everyone he went to each desk and spoke courteously to the security guards in Thai. He carefully stamped each one of the fuming Russian's documents, then he limped out from behind the counter and trundled back smiling to his mistress complete with passport and documents.

Josh touched my arm, I slowly turned to face him slightly dumbfounded by the whole experience. His face had a bovine serenity that reminded me of a masticating bullock. He really was quite sweet in a properly stupid way. Without a shred of irony he said

- "You see what I mean dude. They're lovely people the Thais. That's Buddhism right there; helping out that poor pregnant woman who couldn't even stand. He went out of his way to sort her out; they're just naturals in the service industry. Can you imagine that happening in London? No. It's beautiful in its simplicity man..."

. . . . . . . . . . . . . . .

On the Khao San rd, drinking with Teemo, I had begun to consider the word *'disillusion.'* Disillusion only rears it's ugly head when we allow our lives to become infected with expectation. Teemo was disillusioned because he had allowed himself the expectation that 1989 and the summer of love would last forever. He had made his home here on the Khao San rd because it is a place that purveys the illusion of eternal revelry. Every night it plays the same songs.

Josh was disillusioned with his spirituality; so much so that he had come half way across the world to reconnect with the notion of faith. Me? Well, I had become disillusioned with myself; I hated the useless old drunk that I was becoming. I had abandoned my life and I came here to see something new.

Does this mean that Thailand is full of disillusioned people?

I don't think so. There is much merriment here. The deprivation and the corruption are masked from the ex-pats pretty well; as foreigners, we generally never get to see that side of Thai life. How long that will last I do not know. It is a truly marvelous place, I hope it doesn't lose too much of it's magical craziness. Perhaps the little word I should have unpacked more clearly was "hope."

And what of little Kim Soon?

. . . . . . . . . . . . . . .

The final day of my IEP, I had decided to award the boys, who had genuinely engaged with the program, gifts of encouragement. This was not difficult. In a class of 25 it was clear that only half had paid minimal attention despite my rather cunning use of games and bribery. Kuhn Hao had been an amazingly bright and enthusiastic student, he had consistently proved and improved his natural ability and flair for speaking and writing. I had decided to give him the DVD of 'Star Trek,' as he told me he liked science fiction. Kuhn Jack was boisterous and loud, but he was always first on hand to help organise team activities, so I awarded him a bag of chewy lime hamburgers to share with his team.

Naturally on hearing their names called there was much applause from the others and they seemed genuinely pleased with the gifts.

"The award for best written work goes to Kim Soon."

I noticed from the corner of my eye that during the applause several hands nudge the snoozing boy and he wobbled forward from his chair to collect his Ferrero Rocher. He beamed uncomfortably and then returned to his seat and began rustling through the packet, rather like a hamster. He shared the sweets with others.

After the class had been dismissed he came to my desk as I was packing up my things. Wide-eyed and fully awake he said.

- "The worst about watching the news... Um... That made me really sadder, is that I saw Elizabeth Taylor had died." He said rather glumly.
- "For me she is the only Maggie Pollit, Tennesse Williams will like her I think. Sad. I am sure the aliens will like her."
- "I have no doubt they will Kim Soon."

It somehow wasn't the thing that I had wanted to say. It sounded hollow and empty and it stank of disillusion.

He then left a small folded up piece of paper on my desk and hoicked his enormous ruck sack stuffed with *Milka Cow* accessories onto his back. Again he wobbled for a moment before finding his balance; a serene look of contentment lifted his tiny head. I watched him awkwardly trundle off and in a selfish way I felt quite relieved.

I hope you understand Kim Soon that the world is full of deception, death and murder. Everywhere there is disillusion and people with high expectations are shattered everyday, but that isn't the full story. There are people who see beauty and kindness in everything and they are fortunate to gaze on smiles and laughter. After all, we are human beings and we all make mistakes, that is a fact, and it's the tiny things in life that give us hope.

I opened up the carefully folded piece of paper and on it I read the words:

"Thank you. You have made me very happy. I hope the aliens like you. Kim Soon."

# PART 7 - SUKHUMVIT - FEBRUARY - 2011

I like to think of Thailand as the land of ghosts, because I'm English. We are a race infected by a Gothic sensibility; even in the beautiful sunshine I seek out the shade. Some people call it *the land of smiles,* which it is; others call it *Toyland,* which it is too, but for me it will always be the land of ghosts.

According to local Thai people, we live in a world inhabited by the spirits of our ancestors. In front of every building there is a spirit house made of wood, where they live, and frequently people leave them offerings of orange *Fanta,* and flowers to appease their prankster ways. I have it on good authority (one of the cleaning ladies) that ghosts prefer *Fanta* to *Sprite,* which leads me to believe that our ancestors have a healthy sense of irony.

At the moment Thannon Sukhumvit is awash with ghost houses and empty offices, the signs *'To - Let,'* say it all; in many ways it feels like life has vacated the business centre, I get the sense that something is missing. Bangkok exists between two worlds. It is hard to describe the paradox, one world embraces the modern and the new, the other throws away the past or leaves it hollow, decaying where it stands.

I am sitting in a coffee shop at the base of the Sino-Thai tower looking out onto Thannon Sukhumvit. I am staring at the spirit house in front of the building. It looks ancient but it is not. It is covered with small bottles of red and orange *Fanta.* Even here On Sukhumvit, a monumental sky-scraping centre of business, the old ghosts need placating. I am waiting to attend a job interview at a Japanese business school.

It's funny to think the ghosts have a home here among the ultra-modern, high tech offices. Weirdly, the spirit house does not look out of place with it's intricate ramshackle carving. I am aware that I am staring through tinted glass at a wooden reminder of something otherworldly. Even the most rational and educated people here in Thailand have heard the knockings from the other side, and they are more than happy to share the spectral tale over a glass of Johnny Walker whiskey.

I feel at home with the ghosts.

Perhaps that is why I allowed my co-worker to take me to her medium. Frankly, I was a tad unimpressed. The medium certainly looked the part; she was wizened and crumpled and she reminded me of an old bag of potatoes. She squatted on a tiny stool in the road, just off Thanon Silom, surrounded by incense and sacred objects. She looked at me with her narrow black eyes and said, with almighty gravitas, something I did not understand in Thai. I was transfixed and a little nervous. My friend translated.

- "She ah...She Say you are handsome man. You will have beautiful wife and many beautiful, health children."

My friend then informed her I was gay; at which point she sucked in breath and closed her eyes in reverential communion with the spirit-world. She swayed and convulsed, and the Thai words she spat were clearly dragged from the mouths of the dead; again my friend translated.

- "She ah, she ah, She say the God have forgotten to make you love in this life. Easy for you to get marry, yes, marry. Not love, marry...Sorry."

"Hang on" I said, wrinkling my face in contemplation, "What about the wife and the children?" I felt, in some way that I was cheating on them even though they did not exist. Would I not love them? Am I destined to be a bitter old bastard when I'm older and resent my family? This is advice from the other side? Perhaps she was right, I suppose only a few people ever marry for love. In fact, many of the gay men I know who are getting married are only doing it for financial reasons, or passports, or maybe just the huge party – come to think of it, why does anyone get married anyway?

- "Ah...Yes...You might not find gay you like so you have beautiful wife and beautiful children. Then you find gay in Silom bar. You see? 100 baht. Chaaaaaai."

I am destined to live out my life as a closet case?

Brilliant.

I wonder if I can get any women to settle for that? Probably, this is Thailand. I'd wager most marriages are forged on a heavy foundation of deception. Why on earth am I even considering this nonsense? Still, 100 baht for an identity crisis seems perfectly reasonable to me.

Is it any wonder that educated people in the west view anything spiritual with skeptical cynicism?

I blame Derek Acorah, you have to blame someone so why not him? The man is a fucking idiot. He is a walking advert for lampooning anything paranormal. Him and Yvette Fielding hosted a British TV show, *'Most haunted,'* and are pretty much the reason why all conversations about irrational aspects of our existence now begin and end with the phrase, "what a bag of old shite!" It's like asking, The Krankees to present a serious investigation into paedophilia.

By shutting the magic out of our lives, we in the west sometimes carry our ghosts with us and to some extent this dictates a morose sentimentality which comes to define our culture.

I often wonder how much comfort we obtain from the knowledge that we can split the atom, and does this make us better people?

I don't think so. We seem to find other, darker reasons to internalise our pain, and then we wear it in our hearts because it gives our laboured histories some meaning.

With this in mind visions of young men seem to occupy the periphery of my thoughts, to me they are beautiful specters of the night. Young men have no place in daylight. They should exist in salubrious nightclubs or be wrapped in satin sheets; they should be phantoms of the imagination like...

Ghosts.
Who swim through spectral seas,
They are nothing more than memories...

Suddenly I catch sight of a shadowy figure outside, by the spirit house. I recognize him from somewhere, but where? I cannot recall. He wears dark, heavy clothes and his hair covers his face. He shimmers and flickers because I find it hard to focus in this sunlight. He looks nervous, on edge, and even though he is slender he hides everything from everyone. He does not belong here in Sukhumvit. He fidgets and he always keeps pacing like he fears the immobility. Occasionally he winces like he is hiding a deep, dark pain. His lips are moving and his eyes dart suspiciously from side to side, I try to focus on what he is saying, but it's not making any sense.

The waitress brings my iced latte and I am distracted for a moment, when I look out onto the road again he has vanished. He must have jumped a taxi.

Nothing more than memories...

I take a swig of sweet carnation iced coffee. Perhaps the jolt of pure caffeine, fat and sugar is playing tricks on me. I receive another text from Max. Apparently he wants to know when I will, "make time to play sex."

- "You make me sad why you won't see me :-("

Perhaps it's a cultural, lost in translation, type of thing; however, as far as I'm concerned hip, young, men are anything but honest with me. I had a passionate fling with Max, who is incredibly handsome, and in his mid-twenties. He says he is 24, although I think this may well be a misunderstanding on my part. Even if he is 29, he is too young. Men in their 20's are too young for anyone. I knew, after a few days, he was not for me. But I was flattered by the attention, he kept calling, so... Why not? I had told him I was not interested in being his boyfriend. I had been harsh but honest.

Maybe he had not understood?

I was defeated by his smile and charm. It really is the most amazing feeling to wake up next to a beautiful body in the Bangkok sunshine. I touched his supple skin and knew he was ephemeral. He was just a fleeting vision that briefly permeated my existence; still, I had tasted a new part of life through him, the exchange was intentionally brief and mutually beneficial.

Within a few days the real Max had appeared, and I was reminded of just how arrogant beautiful men in their 20's can be; add to that the fact that Max knew he was incredibly handsome, et voila! Ladies and gentlemen I give you a man who looks at himself in the mirror during sex. Even though I have a king size bed there isn't enough room for me, Max and his ego to frolic on that mattress.

I adore the lack of intimacy,
He keeps me at a distance,
It is where I long to be,
Severed by a smile.

Beautiful Thai people have many "gigs."

I'm not talking about karaoke, which goes without saying, but lovers who provide them with something; dates, sex, money, holidays etc. I love it. I think it's a particularly civilised way of going about the whole coupling experience. Knowing this, I still can't quite understand the deception employed in maintaining this liberal attitude. It all seems quite incongruous. They seem to juggle these affairs with the utmost discretion.

I was under no illusion that Max would be any different. One day he told me he was going home to rest, and on leaving my work in Silom that evening, I saw him having dinner with a rich, fat old American. The American looked visibly mortified - what an amateur. I was totally gracious and introduced myself and Max informed me Bob had just flown in and apparently they were old friends.

Bob was definitely an old friend.

He was in his 70's, at least.

Bob had clearly had a little too much plastic surgery and I was not altogether sure whether he was trying to smile or was suffering from a severe case of wind. I chatted kindly for a while and said I would see Max around, then I left.

Later that night I was woken by a drunk Max who continuously rang my phone, he was downstairs in the lobby of my condo. Clearly Bob had not paid up, so I let him in. He said it was my fault that he was late and I should have stayed with him and Bob. I just told him not to lie about this anymore because, frankly, it insulted my intelligence; plus, I really didn't care. So Max got naked (trust me, he can be forgiven a lot for that), switched on the TV and cracked open a beer. He ranted and shouted,

- "This is all your fault, why haven't you got any nice glasses in your shitty condo?"
- "Why don't you ever iron my shirts for work?"

He then passed out on my bed.

Hilarious.

It was like looking at a younger version of myself; except I had never blown a decrepit American for cash, also I had always ironed my own shirts.

The next morning he woke late for his work on Sukhumvit, he was grumpy, hung-over and handsome. The goodbye was final. I knew he belonged to the night and I was discovering a bright new day. To Max, I suppose, I didn't exist during the daylight hours. I was a passive receiver of his texts, I was a form of lunchtime entertainment on slow days. I assumed that was it. Then the barrage of calls and texts. He loved me and me alone.

- "I see nobody else!"

Naturally; I ignored the texts, not because I was playing games, but because I'm a drama queen, and as such, I feel that one should never taint a sweet adieu with spineless begging. It ruins the pathos. Have none of these young Thai boys seen *Casablanca?*

. . . . . . . . . . . . . .

Isn't it odd that in these days of technological convenience, even the most basic social interaction can be delivered over a distance with the touch of a button. So many people think this is a good thing, but I still maintain that this is odd. It suits the shy and the lonely. The disconnection between human interaction and physical contact is almost complete. We all exist as avatars in a virtual world. We are phantom manifestations hidden behind a barrage of text that defines us more than our physical beings.

Suddenly I shiver.

It is nothing to do with the air-conditioning or the iced latte. There are many cliches used to describe this sensation. It is a phenomenon with which we are all familiar. The hairs tingle on the back of the neck and something, a chill, makes the eyes widen and the heart pound. I twitch in anticipation of seeing the thing that was moving but already it is gone; almost like a ghost, a shadow dancing on the wall.

Maybe it's too much caffeine? I laugh to myself, too much caffeine? Was I not the man who once drank rock-stars under the table? I was indeed, and now I sketch out like a total amateur from one too many lattes.

Did I see something?

I see the figure once again and feel a sharp twinge in my spine. It is something remembered, an old pain that lingers deep within the fiber of my being. I see the figure by the spirit house dressed in black with long hair. He is pacing and looks too scared to stop, even for a second, he must keep moving. I remember him from Liverpool many years ago. He hated himself. He had been paralyzed for months and had become lost in a seizure of pain. During his immobility every minute played out like an hour and so he learned to re-evaluate time. He could not bear his broken body, so he withdrew from the world and took refuge inside his mind, there he created the most beautiful fictions. He wove so many vibrant ballets from the bare motifs of inertia. He dreamed of becoming a rock-star. He prayed to a God that he did not believe in and begged for the chance to put all of this suffering on to a stage. He would scream his songs from the very depths of his frustration and exorcise this demon.

As quickly as he appeared he vanishes behind the spirit house.

Was it him? I'm sure it was.

Why would he be here?

Unsettled by this vision I feel stiffled and I begin to pace. I rise and pretend to look out of the window but I am walking, I am moving and I stretch my fingers, the memory of suffering dissipates into the present.

I become aware of the lady boy who is sitting, knitting at the table to my right. She looks out of place. Yet like the spirit house her eccentricity moulds into the modern surroundings. I am strangely fascinated by her appearance. She has taken to wearing too much skin whitening cream, so her face has a ghoulish look that glows like a mask of consumption. Something about her deathly stare reminds me of an old queen I once knew in Liverpool. He wore too much fake tan. He looked equally disconnected from his environment but, like the lady-boy, he was of it. Nature makes a home for everything, even the oddest creature, even me.

My telephone rings its annoyingly shrill ring-tone, if only I had paid attention, I would know how to change it. The number is unknown so it isn't Max. Max would never use anyone's phone but his, even in an emergency. I answer.

- "Ah yes. You Mr. Yes. I am calling from Geos. Are you on the outside looking in?"

This is a surreal conversation, it all feels existentially fractured, like a David Lynch film. Whoever this woman is she's right; metaphysically speaking, I am on the outside looking in.

- "Um, yes, I think I am."
- "Okay, okay, good. Before you there is a door. Open it and come inside."

It occurs to me that I am already inside. She must think I'm mental.

- "Actually I'm inside. I'm definitely inside, by the coffee shop. Having a coffee. Inside."

I'm spooked for the first time in years.

- "The manager, she have another meeting so can you wait downstairs in coffee-shop?"
- "Certainly. I shall be here, many thanks for calling."

Another latte it is then.

Sugar and condensed milk and caffeine, that should do the trick.

The ladyboy is rather butch and peers at me from behind her busy needles. I feel like she holds me in contempt, even though she probably doesn't.

She sees the fraud of a man, in a suit, who quivers at the sight of a ghost.

Then from the corner of my eye I see another ghost. He struts like a peacock and he relishes every movement. He strides, like he rules the world, towards the spirit house. I notice a dull sheen to his eyes, red rimmed, they reveal the faintest trace of green. He hates himself. His confidence is all a sham, a performance. He wears dark skin-tight clothes beneath a fitted white jacket. His hair is tousled short and it shows lovely bone structure covered with wrinkled skin.

I can assure you these are not reflections, or anything as two dimensional as that. Neither are they simple hallucinations. They have a body and a presence that defies all rational explanation. They are as real to me as the image in your mirror. Sepia stained, like old photographs, the edges are quite blurred, yet they are real.

They are the shadows of old memories that plague me.

I must be dreaming.

The lady boy shuffles silently and I am distracted by her strangeness. I wonder what ghosts visit her in the days when even the simplest act of finding a job can be so perplexing. She radiates an ethereal calmness and takes a sip from an iced tea and washes down a handful of hormones.

What are we?

What have we become?

I remember the long haired man in Liverpool once sat with a handful of pills seeking redemption. It was his decision not to become a ghost but to live, and now he is unrecognisable, transformed by circumstance.

I look out of the window onto the busy Sukhumvit road. It must be break time, as the streets are filling up with petite, wafer-thin girls all carrying plastic bags of food. Everyone is always eating. The consumption is corporeal, of the body; it's not ephemeral, of the soul.

I see Max.

Is it Max?

Yes... I think it is, the memories of hot nights on sweat stained sheets fill my mind. Carnal images of skin on skin sliding and grinding. It feels like this body of mine, the one that was broken, was fixed for a purpose, to revel in that moment of coupling. For the briefest of moments it had meaning.

He walks towards the Sino-Thai tower, with colleagues, and he looks so different in his pristine shirt and tie. The heavy sun skips from his almond skin, and there is something vital about him, his black hair shines like opals. He walks with pride. He knows he is loved he is confident. I am pretty sure his mother must dedicate her life to ironing his shirts; I know I wouldn't, what spirits lurk within her mind? Just how much has she sacrificed for her little Max?

I think for a second that his eyes meet mine, and there it is, a flicker of something that mattered for a moment but then disappeared into the shade. I can smell coconut. Fresh coconut that he would rub into his skin on hot nights after showering, the scent would linger on my sheets.

He doesn't see me, though I am right in front of him, separated by vaguely tinted glass.

He looks right through me and I know I do not exist in his world. To Max I belong to the night.

He doesn't even recognise me.

. . . . . . . . . . . . . .

I finish my coffee and realise it is time for me to face the interview. I picture a sterile atmosphere, pristine and unfamiliar, an environment so removed from the Bangkok I have grown to love. What will it be like working for a Japanese company? No doubt it will be alien and different, like another world. The only thing I know about Japanese businessmen, here in Bangkok, is their insatiable appetite for the Bangkok prostitutes. Apparently the local girls refer to them as "Sam-Sam," the three threes. Three inches, three minutes and three thousand baht.

At least working for a Japanese company I will have some security, they are prosperous and effective in business, none of this running around begging for legitimacy. In my mind, the Japanese system appears to be something industrial and dependable. As a rational westerner I have put my faith in the security of civilisation and order. I have no need of a spirit house. I can say with some certainty that there are no ghosts and everything can be explained.

I have read somewhere that ghosts are memories that are stored in the cells of the nervous system. Like diseases that can be cured, and disasters that can be averted, they are nothing more than glitches that have no real power over civilised human beings. We have strength and order. We have left the darkness of our natural pasts behind. We say we are not scared of ghosts and yet we keep on moving, terrified of our own inertia. If I am honest, I will always be uncomfortable embracing the stillness.

I pick up my portfolio and CV's and I gather my thoughts. So many lives lived, so many references to a life I can't forget. I briefly glimpse the rock-star and the long haired boy by the spirit house. They are looking for a home and they belong to the past.

I was broken once but now I'm fixed.
That is what we do when we things get broken,
They are fixed,
We spend our lives industriously mending,
What's left behind, is just the spirit fading.

There are so many people who suffer much more than the boy who ran away. He was only lost. There are people who lose everything and still maintain an awe inspiring dignity.

Here is my ghost, my demon, my mirror. Does it really matter? Why not believe in ghosts? Even if they don't exist, we can make them as real as the gilded spirit houses, or the lives lived in fear. I head towards the lift and see my future not my past. I meet a man in uniform who is of this world. He clicks his heels and salutes my approach, I'll never get used to that, and my phone vibrates.

A text from Max... I have to laugh. I don't even read it.

I was the boy who ran until he could not run,
I lived in fear.
I was the rock-star who sang until the song was sung;
I hid my fear.
Now, at last, I live alone and have no fear.

# PART 6 - HUALAMPHONG - JANUARY – 2011

Life, like literature, often demands a happy ending. With that in mind I had decided to have a massage near Thanon Silom at my favourite emporium, "Adonis Massage and Day Spa."

Such talented boys.

They really know what they are doing; with their oily fingers, they soothe away my troubles in a manner that is almost transcendental. Feeling rather zen, I make my way to work.

It's strange the things we incorporate into our daily routines, and how such things come to define us.

How do I define myself?

English? Cornish? Working class? Gay? Straight? White? All of these terms are meaningless on their own. I could be any number of different combinations of these same things and be a completely different person. I adore the random combination of DNA and circumstance that renders generalisations completely pointless; in many ways, the exceptions have now become the new standard.

When observing or writing, sometimes I like to allow the characters voices to infect their narrative, to a certain degree they speak for themselves. In an effort to empathise with people I cannot empathise with, I present an objective observation with a subjective analysis, and a balance is always hard to find

It is not always easy to see the love in some characters. The medium is constricting, but it is my hope that the message is conveyed. In doing this, to some extent, I lose my own voice. Who am I? What do I feel? These stories I am writing are an attempt to reclaim my voice, and to a certain degree they should be seen as rather indulgent; in my defense, I do spend the majority of my time focusing on the lives of other people, so it is healthy to maintain a balance, and keep a diary.

Take today for example. It is sunny and hot and I am on my way to work at a well respected all boys school here in Bangkok. I am hoping that they will sponsor my work permit, they have assured me they will, but then – so have many schools here in Thailand.

The morning massage has left me floating. I have taken the sky-train and MRT and the carriages are chilled to perfection; so, I do not feel the heat. Here I am in one of the hottest countries in the world, slightly cold, even though I wear a sleeveless pullover to appear smart for work.

I rather like my life at the moment. I feel a zen-like calm; which, for me is the ultimate antithesis to my former self. I had grown so accustomed to my own neurosis in London that I nurtured it like an old friend.

I chose to live.

I worked hard to become qualified and still I work hard to pay for my qualification; something that has meaning here, amid the pandemonium of Asia.

I arrive at Hua Lamphong station and the heat dries my throat and makes me swallow. The sweat soaks my shirt to my spine and, slightly uncomfortable, I'm suddenly conscious that I must smell like a massage parlour. I head out into the glare and look for cool salvation on the back of a scooter bike taxi.

We all have our foibles, our fantasies, our fetishes. I happen to enjoy riding on the back of scooter-taxis. The bikers tear along and weave through traffic at an alarming speed and I experience a freedom I have not felt since I was young. The breeze is warm and such a trip alleviates the stiffling claustrophobia of Bangkok traffic; a notorious mechanical beast that grinds its way through the city.

It is a short ride to my school from Hua Lamphong, and yet culturally it's a million miles away from the tourist hub and the traveller cafe's.

The journey is a joy, it's an adventure in itself. We zoom past canals and bridges, we skip onto pavements and hurtle down the wrong side of the road. I kid you not, I love this town, it's bonkers.

The school I am currently working for is an all boys school in the grounds of a temple. It is full of boys from 11, I think, to about 18, but it's impossible to tell; being a foreigner, I am pretty much left outside the loop of most things. I receive my time-table, my lesson plans, and then I am left to fend for myself. Thai people in general look much younger than their European counterparts, which makes ageing the boys even harder.

I have discovered that there are a huge number of gay students here, that became obvious after my first week. I know that teenage Thai boys can be slightly camper than their European counterparts, but even with this in mind, it's pretty clear the boys in this school are definitely bender friendly. It's like being in an Asian working class version of "*Brideshead*

*Revisited,"* but with more *Lady Gaga* and less tawdry angst.

At first I thought the boys were taking the piss. I have a certain flamboyance that many would consider camp; So, naturally I assumed that all of the boys were mimicking my mannerisms as a typical school yard joke.

But no. I had alighted at Bumtown central.

After I had taught my first Matayon 6 class, complete with a table of young lady-boys, I realized that I was actually the butchest man in the room, and I was wearing a polkadot tie. The lady-boys in waiting sized me up, decided I was okay for a *farrang*, and then proceeded to put on make-up and flirt with me outrageously.

Trying to describe all this by European standards is quite impossible, and it is this simple observation that fills me with a calm and it inspires me to write a short memoir.

Here I sit, in the grounds of the most beautiful temple, waiting to teach a class of young Thai chaps the subtle intricacies of active and passive sentence construction; knowing in my heart that they will inevitably make jokes about being a bottom, when suddenly I feel a wave of regret. Why is this?

The trigger, you see, was watching a Tuk-tuk driver bring his son to school this morning and hug him; even though the boy had taken to wearing a rather gaudy shade of blusher; electric red is the fashion, there was love and pride in the fathers eyes. Visions of the family meeting flow into my mind. I can see father and grandfather shrug and sway their heads in disappointment. They would disapprove of their mincing boy. The mother of course would weep a little at the thought of her beautiful son not finding a ravishing Siamese princess to give them the fair skinned grandchildren of which they had dreamed. The younger brother would no doubt giggle pick his nose and demand a Nintendo Wii in compensation for his elder brothers sparkling new platform shoes. Then the matter would be done; Finished, and father would continue to drive his new daughter to school and wonder how he was going to afford a Nintendo Wii. Secretly, I suspect he would be relieved that he would only have to shell out for a pair of boobs in the future, and not the whole wife and wedding.

We have become so used to the archetypal distant father in European literature and society that conduct between male generations is scrutinized beyond all reasonable context.

We have become so familiar with the concept of the misery memoir, that the notion of a broken family has become, in some way, acceptable. Why shouldn't a father hug his son? Why shouldn't a 16 year old boy choose to wear make-up?

My first memory of my father is one of sadness and trauma and hatred and it is something I have never left behind. It was violence and shouting and I disappeared next door to our neighbour's room, and we danced on her bed to David Bowie records. There I experienced an escapism and joy that will never leave me, and frequently it brings me to tears; even now, when I'm the other side of the world, surrounded by smiles and sunshine.

I cannot remember the details, and why should I? The effects have been bad enough without having to relive the scenarios again and again. Being treated like a bastard by your legitimate father is evil, it will drive any man to madness. I will never settle or feel comfortable having a family, or a relationship for that matter. My friends and my students are my family. I can enjoy their company and then disappear back into the darkness of my room to plan for their futures; their lives. Their hopes and their dreams mean more to me than my own, my dreams mean nothing.

There is great suffering and tragedy here in Thailand, yet with regard to the majority of Asian people that I have met, the family is a solid foundation. The difference is noticeable. Autonomy and self governance have taken their toll on many western families which fracture and propagate independence in the name of freedom, but at what cost? Even the poorest and the lowliest boys who come to this school with their tattered, patched up shoes have the love of a father.

And it is this that drags me back into the past.

After the drama came the laughter; as it should, and I remember my mother and I moving to a farm in the middle of nowhere which was falling down and had holes in the roof. It was a beautiful cottage, 400 years old, and we would delight in telling stories about the witches and the ghosts who had lived there in the past. We had many friends. We were liked. In my past there were beautiful people, and beautiful times. I must have annoyed my friends quite regularly with my tantrums and my tears, manifestations of shock, but all of this was framed with laughter and music.

Pop music.

I loved the rock and roll, and when I had free time I would put on records and dance. Disco, heavy metal, pop; it was all medicine to me and looking back, as I am, all I can remember are sunny days in fields, riding in tractors to barns to play and to dance to rock and roll music.

This of course is not the complete picture.

We forget the day to day when writing a memoir, as I have been told, our memories are always selective. So, do I mention the cold winters?

The freezing house? The fact we had no money and were denied adequate maintenance? Who cares. It was grim, but my mother and I made the best of it, she my friends, like her mother, is a credit to our race.

And what of my father?

Those times are filled with hatred and repulsion. I remember he tried on numerous occasions to form some kind of relationship. He even felt the need to attempt to incorporate me into his new family. The damage had been done and I always felt like a bastard, something in the way, someone to be pitied. I pity him now because I understand more about how life works, and that is bad. It's a shameful notion to pity your father.

Not here.

In the sun.

Surrounded by boisterous young fellows, tumbling and stumbling their way through adolescence. They are so happy and when I was their age I was...

School became my home, and Primary to secondary I would revel in the time that I would spend there. When the family is destroyed, people learn to love their institutions. They put in them a sense of permanence that is ultimately unfounded. I met many exciting new friends and experienced all the drama and the joy of teenage life; there was sadness, and joy and girlfriends. Yes, girlfriends, I had many girlfriends and even in that respect I was a ridiculous drama queen. I would lavish them with tapes and sweet words, and think that every kiss was eternal and every song by *The Bangles* held the key to our future happiness; so yes, naturally I was bullied.

It turns out that here in Bangkok, *"Manic Monday,"* is my waking dream. I play it in the gym every morning.

I remember a girl called Nicola.

She had green eyes and I thought that she loved me.

She didn't.

She's not stupid.

She was only in it for the cheeky finger.

It's nearly time to start my lesson for the M2 class, one of my largest classes, it is filled to the brim with young chaps who are, I think, 14-16 nobody will tell me exactly. There are close to 60 boys in the class, but nobody will tell me exactly. They are my favourite class, so much fun and they actually wish to learn. I'm trying to imagine a state classroom of 60+ English boys in London; it would never happen. Some of the foreign teachers here in Bangkok complain and moan about the dire state of the public schools. They are usually Australian, from New Zealand or privately educated. I think the purveying attitude is fun, and that's probably not a good thing academically; however, it does go a long way socially.

Fun.

I quickly learned to adapt my academic teaching practices into a workable model that at least achieves some involvement with the language; but more often than not, teaching here in this school feels like crowd control.

I remember fun. Will I ever experience that again?

There were clumsy mistakes and beatings, but yes, there was fun. There was *Bon-jovi* and *Guns and Roses,* the odd cheeky finger, the drama with girlfriends, and the fumbles with boyfriends, and I wonder if these boys are living these dramas?

I see some boys from my class.

They are clumsy;

Tumbling they fumble and their bodies are a jumble of ineptitude;
They look a mess and yet they're happy as they are,
Un-tucked, and such a shambles.
Let their bodies find their fingers
And their grace will come in time.
Wistfully they scatter through their days,
But for now,
The clatter of the broken things they shatter
leaves behind a messy muddle - that is fine.

This is what my father took from me. This ability to trust in others, the ability to tumble and know that I will be caught. He selfishly chose to ruin other people's lives. He fucked up, and perhaps I should forgive him but I can't. He has left me cold.

I remember a young French student who came to our school to speak French and patch up the shoddy job imposed on us by Madame Way, a neurotic woman with a tendency to weep when we were boisterous. The French student's name eludes me. I remember she wore stripes, blue and white which I liked, they seemed so elegant and carefree. On the day of her departure I gave her a *Curly-Wurly* and wished her a safe journey back to her friends.

Her friends.

I wonder who they are?

Did I sing for them?

Did I really sing with a French band?

How on earth did that happen?

The roof of the temple next to where I sit is the brightest of oranges with ornate fingers of gold that stretch out to the Buddha. I think that they remind me of my fingers when I dance. Stretching back and curving in shapes of communication not clenched in fists but splayed, they are open.

I am from a land of fists, so I clench my mind and now I focus on the moment. I feel pregnant with possibility, yet constricted by something unseen. A young monk, brown and slightly bloated, wearing pristine orange robes passes by and smiles and he says in perfect English, "How are you?"

"Oh Yes I'm fine!" I reply, "just waiting for my class."

He stops and produces an i-phone from his robes and hands it to me.

- "We have a group on Facebook if you'd like to join, the students like you. You're from the West-country I believe?"

I take the phone and look at a small Facebook page for the school. He continues to smile, "But you hide it well," he says.

Now I am impressed.

- "Actually I'm from London, but I have many friends in the west-country."

I lie, why not, that'll teach him to be clever. Try and fool me with your mystical monk ways.

- "I could have sworn you had the lilt of a Cornish accent?"

First lesson you should learn here is never lie to a monk, people lie to them all the time, they are used to it and they can spot it a mile away.

- "My mother's from Cornwall."
- "A beautiful part of the world so I've been told."

"Indeed it is." I say. "You should go there," I have of course by now relinquished all pretensions in my accent, so the, "there," betrays a subtle rolling "r."

"Perhaps." He smiles again. "So what brings you all the way here?"

- "Well, I graduated and love language, so I thought I'd like to travel and..."

My story trails off into nothing and I find myself rather uncomfortably looking at my folder, and realize that I am opening and closing the bindings for no particular reason at all. "To be honest I have no idea."

- "I didn't say you had to have a reason. I was merely interested, that's all. The students like you and it's rare we have a foreigner they like; far too many people come here to run away from their lives, they are escaping something, you see; so, they bring nothing but contempt, they are not teachers."

Has he hacked my Facebook account?

Am I that transparent?

Am I running away?

Then it dawns on me that I'm not running away or escaping. He is not talking about me, he is talking to me, it is a minor epiphany that touches me. This is my home and I am not afraid anymore. At the moment I'm a good teacher. All too often we blame our pasts for everything and we forget our present purpose.

I wasted years of my life blaming my past.

Our sense of adventure should not be born of fear, hatred or the violence of the past. We should not have to run away. Perhaps I should re-write the narratives of our Christian pilgrimage. It would be a story where enlightenment is not a journey to a promised land, it is a place that exists here, in the moment.

- "Anyway I apologize for disturbing you from your work, I shall let you get on."

I hand him back his i-phone just as it vibrates into life. He answers with a cheery, "Sawadee krap!" and waves and wanders off back into the temple chirping merrily about Facebook.

. . . . . . . . . . . . . .

What a beautiful life so far from London. The brilliant sun shines down and I see greenery that is cared for and pollution that is discarded carelessly; everywhere, the subtlest of contradictions makes me happy.

In my mind I am striving for the thing that lets me stay; a permit: a visa; and it is then I realize it is only me who can make this happen. For the time being, this is my family and my home, there can be nowhere else. What's left for me in Europe needs some changing, and I alone cannot do that.

My friends are many, but my demons have the power.

I am my fathers son and until I can respect that I am barren.

The UK is not the place for me. I equate it with him; to me it has become a sad place, pedaling history and malcontent.

There it is you see, too much dissection. I sit here in the most beautiful place on the planet and all that I can do is tumble backwards, forever picking over carcasses, I pick and pick. I should just let it be.

Hang on.

Did I just meet a monk who speaks perfect English and has a gay pop anthem as the ring-tone on his iphone?

At what point did that ever happen to my father?

I shut him out for a good reason. He has missed all of the good stuff.

A young chap from my class stops over to see me, Kuhn Kaen. He is 16 and bright and he likes English. He is adorable. He is always tucked and impeccable and polite, his shorts and shoes are proudly neat. He has a crush on me, I think, which I respect as I'm his teacher.

I had a crush on many of my teachers.

I had many unrequited loves.

I sabotaged true love to keep things simple.

I am bathed in the green and gold and white of a beautiful Buddhist temple. It shines out in my eyes and excites my heart, like the first party I ever gatecrashed. I think I relish this moment more. I am not the man my father is, so why should I not celebrate this fact? That's a good thing right?

Kuhn Kaen gives me a solemn wai, his eyes peeking at me from behind slender fingers.

- "Hello. Mr Teacher sir. Next week we move to M3 and we would like to say how good it is to have...Have been having you."

It would appear that my work on the past tense has been causing some confusion; however, I do seem to have successfully given my students the ability to communicate in *double entendre*s. How queer.

- "It has been a joy teaching you Mr Kaen, your English is very good and I'm sure it will improve."

He smiles and clears his throat.

- "We have buy you some sweet...To say thank you Mr Teacher."

I look down and another boy appears with a collection of assorted sweets, he is tiny, a spindly bundle of smiles and his uniform hangs about him in a manner that reminds me of my own childhood. Suddenly I hear my mother's voice, as clear as day, "Stop whinging! You'll grow into it!"

I cannot recall this particular chaps name and I curse my lack of observation. I shall refer to him as, Mr Spindly. Has he avoided my class altogether? Perhaps he hopes to obtain his pass from me by bribing me with sweets? I know their cunning ways these smiling chaps, and who can blame them? It is the way of life. I look at the sweets. They are *"Love bars,"* emblazoned with the English phrase, *"Love you forever!"* Apparently such a sentiment in Asia can be expressed with a strawberry chew - written in English. I am touched. I seem to remember having the same feeling about a *'Curly-wurly'* many years ago...

Kuhn Kaen looks down at me wide eyed and urgently pushes the other boys hands saying something in Thai which causes tension. The sweets tumble onto my folder and my eyes follow them. *"Love you forever,"* they say as they tumble, and I recall uttering those very words to a girl called Nicola.

*"Love you forever."*

Easy words to write, easy words to say, for a sentimental old queen like me, they are impossible to feel, and that's life.

Kuhn Kaen berates the smaller chap, who recoils and raises his spindly hands in apology.

- "Sorry Ajarn Sir.
- "That's alright, no need to apologize, you didn't have to buy me sweets, that is very kind of you, are you prepared for your tests next week?"

I speak clearly and slowly, not loudly and patronizingly like so many teachers do here, I try to speak with kindness.

Mr Spindly shuffles nervously and covers his smile. That's a no from him then. Kuhn Kaen purses his lips and it is visibly apparent that he is trying to form his words correctly.

- "I think so Ajarn Sir. The English have a hard one, but I am hoping to lick it."

I'm in constant shock and disbelief. It is horrific. This is really not my fault. It's like watching a horrendous racist sketch from the mid-seventies.

- "Now Kuhn Kaen, that's an American phrase, if you use it in this context, 'to lick,' is not the main verb, it is, 'to hope,'so the phrase is, 'hope to get it licked!'"
- "Ah yes. 'Get it licked'... The English has a hard one but I am hoping to get it licked."

This sounds even more ridiculous. It would be rude to laugh, it would shatter his confidence.

- "That's better Kuhn Kaen. Make sure you practice everyday. You have a firm grip on the English language."

He looks somewhat baffled and bemused.

Such confusion doesn't suit him, it makes him look oddly stern and ancient. Perhaps I should grade my language a little more and think of terms he'll understand? Less confusing idioms. "I have..." He stumbles, "I have... A..Fiwm...Gwip?"

- "It's an expression Kuhn Kaen, a colloquialism, it doesn't matter."

- "I hawe... Wah.. Vah... Have a firm gwip?"
- "Um, better, but it means you understand English."
- "I have a firm grip...I have a firm grip..."
- "That's right Kuhn Kaen, but it's better to say I understand, better, understand is better."
- "I have a firm grip. I have a firm grip!"
- "Yeah, better to say, 'I understand' You understand English. That's better. "

He clenches his fist and shakes it at me while smiling and nodding. It's hideous. I'm not doing this on purpose, I swear; It's really not me. I hope he doesn't go around bragging to everyone that he has *"a firm grip."*

- "I will Ajarn. Understand. I have a firm grip. Will you be here next semester?"

He looks at me in earnest and I feel slightly saddened at the thought of leaving, "I don't think so, I need to find a full-time placement, job, work. You see, your school does not offer teachers full time work. I cannot work here every day."

I look down at my folder and as stealthily as a cat the spindly boy has neatly stacked my *Love forever* bars into piles according to flavour, blue raspberry is the best apparently, as it's on top.

Kuhn Kaen turns to his companion and there is an intensely serious exchange in Thai that defies my comprehension. I have the distinct impression they are discussing something of great importance. Kuhn Kaen looks back at me and says,

- "Will you stay later this evening? We have made a dance to support our team. Football yes! You like Arsenal from London! We make a dance like Lady Ga-Ga. We work vely hard."

Inside I am laughing. Is it just me or is this whole thing preposterous? This really is my life now.

"Of course, I would love to see it, I will be there." They grin and nod excitedly, Mr Spindly says,

- "We dance vely good! Will you be going home to see your Pah in London?"

And there you have it; twenty years, thousands of miles and countless fictions and songs written, I am no further away from the truth than when I left. I dip my eyes momentarily and that is enough to alert Kuhn Kaen to this intrusion. He elbows his friend, who retorts in Thai and looks at me again, with an innocence that is quite disarming.

- "I wish you a safe journey back to your family. You will be seeing your Pah yes?"

I graciously accept this complement in the spirit that it is given. Who is this Mr Spindly fellow anyway? I suppose it is quite natural for him to assume that my father plays a part in my life.

Kuhn Kaen approaches me cautiously and rests his hand on my shoulder,

- "you are sad, you must miss your Pah, but you will see him soon, yes?"

I rise and his hand falls away as I collect my folder and I put the stack of sweets in my battered old shoulder bag. I focus on the lesson ahead. I focus on the future. I focus on the fact that I have sung my songs and now I fill my days with merriment and sunshine. I am all of this, not because I am my fathers son, but despite the fact I am his son. I will never understand the workings of the people closest to me.

"Perhaps..." I say, a wry smile returns to my lips.

- "Now, come along, we must go to class and then you must get ready for your dance... Which *Lady Gaga* song is it? Don't tell me, is it *Bad Romance*? Ah yes, that's my favourite too. Don't use too much of that skin whitening foundation Kaen, in this heat you'll get spots."

Perhaps here in Bangkok I wouldn't make such a bad father.

So, to sum up, I still have no full time placement. I have no money. It has all gone off road, but I really don't care, I think I might actually be stumbling on something much more profound.

At least I'm not drinking my life away in a shit Camden pub.

I think that tomorrow I shall go out and buy a copy of *Lady Gaga's* CD and smash it up into a million pieces in the hope that I never have to hear it again.

I shall wear my French breton, blue striped shirt, and I shall eat fresh pineapple and teach some crazy kids the basics of our language. I can tell you for sure that tomorrow will be a beautiful day filled with giggles. It has been an odd journey, but I think I might have found a place that I belong. I feel comfortable being on the outside, peering in on life, I think it suits me.

# PART 5 - SILOM - DECEMBER – 2010

- "It's not like that at all, he really is the most genuine fellow, he runs his own business for goodness sake,"

pleaded William, pathetically pushing up his spectacles that had started to slide down his nose. The confounded heat proved too much for a portly old chap like him, and he had taken to perspiring into numerous handkerchiefs shipped over from *Harrods* by his rather matronly younger sister. Even the most hardy pilgrims, it would appear, require a few comforts from home.

- "Runs his own business? But he's a prostitute man! It's his job to make you fall in love with him!"

William accepted this lashing in the spirit it was given and rubbed his scarlet cheeks, maybe he was being an old fool? He looked at the younger chap who was scoffing a cold *Chang* and even managed to appear quite lucid, despite the obvious bulging eyes and salivating drunken poise.

- "You've never met him and besides he's from a perfectly respectable Thai family, creative chap, he merely accepts donations from wealthy foreign patrons, of which I am one..."
- "He's a prostitute!"

Once again, when confronted by such crass insensitivity, William Hewitt felt he should defend the honour of his young companion.

- "He has never deceived me, and if he says that he loves me then naturally I am to believe him. He only ever sleeps with me..."

This elicited a somewhat condescending look from John who shook his head from side to side while still managing to fix his eyes forward into his glass.

- "...He says that he loves me and I suppose, for want of a better word, I love him too. There. I've said it. I love him."

John scoffed a little too hard on the final swig of beer and lifted a finger to order another; damned *Chang,* he thought, it will be my undoing.

- "I don't mean to be rude William, but exactly how old is he?"

Whoever had designed these bar stools had clearly not had William Hewitt in mind or indeed any of the clientele who frequented *"Rich-pickings,"* here in the quiet little shambles that was Soi 2/1. He lumbered uncomfortably in the stool and lent forward on to the bar trying to settle and somehow he managed to avoid the rather embarrassing stare that John had now adopted.

- "Well obviously he's quite a bit younger than me, but they say that love is blind... I just don't think that Thai people have an issue with age like us British folk, they respect the aged and there's a certain dignitas one gets when one is older. In England of course the old are imprisoned in homes and forgotten by everyone, it's rather savage don't you think?"

John had remained motionless while listening to this awkward monologue and was not fooled by such a ludicrous distraction,

- "How old is he?"
- "He's 24. Now I know in England such an affair would seem ridiculous; but out here, when you've been here as long as I have, you will see that the people don't view age in the same way that we do, as he says, *'age is only a number!'*"

Why William had felt the need to apologise to this jumped up drunken oik at the bar he didn't know. He continued to validate his reasoning with spluttered out sentences.

- "He's on his way here now, you can meet him if you like, he has been working on a difficult painting, something rather gruesome in oils I believe, and should be here in a few minutes; I'd be delighted if you could join us for a drink."

He found a suitable position on the stool at last and resumed adjusting his spectacles.

John was never one to refuse the invitation of a drink, so his rather superior stance on William's relationship had disappeared into a friendly order at the bar.

William instantly regretted his decision to Invite John to join him, he felt he was in some way buying the man's approval but he was sure that upon meeting young Gee, he would be vindicated. Secretly, William was looking forward to proving this drunken idiot wrong; a completely ungracious reason for asking a man to drink with you, but there you have it.

John was a wiry man in his thirties who had left London on account of the fact that he could no longer afford to drink there anymore. He had given other reasons to the few friends and acquaintances that bothered to inquire as to the purpose of his move, but the fact of the matter remained, he liked to get pissed.

Everything was just too expensive in London, so he had sold his flat and headed to the land of smiles, where *Chang* was cheap and in abundance, and there were always handsome boys who were impressed by a fading mullet hairdo. He considered himself something of a maverick, despite the rather obvious fact that he was just another drunken old poof.

Another pilgrim burned by the light of the sun.

It had all been going so well for John, he had owned his own business and had been living with a demanding Indian boyfriend in a flat in Brixton. Then, one day, it suddenly dawned on him that all he actually liked doing was getting pissed and putting the world to rights, and it was probably the Tory party's fault that he couldn't do that.

The Indian left with all of the electrical goods in a maelstrom of smashing plates and passionate posturing. Slowly, but surely, John's life became a non-stop piss up in Brixton. He hung about with the punks and the tattoo artists, and suddenly thought this made him a revolutionary. He wanted to be an outsider, a drunken poet who saw the truth. London had become far too expensive to live the life of a pretentious drunk. Here in Bangkok, he could become the maverick he had always dreamed. It was, for him, the perfect place to construct his disconnected facade.

"What news from London?" asked William, which suddenly snatched John away from his befuddled memoir and back into a hazy reality.

- "It's all gone to shit!"

He was getting drunker than he should, but he thought an impassioned response might be entertaining for the old man.

- "By that I mean everything is being sold down the river. The bankers are stealing from everyone and the Tories are finding new ways of making the rich richer and the poor poorer and nobody seems to care."

As he was becoming more and more inebriated, his native estuary accent descended into a fake London brawl, he was conscious of this and considered it quite *cool.* The Indian boyfriend had said it had made him sound like an idiot.

William was not impressed, it would have been fine for Winston Churchill or Princess Margaret to have said such a thing but for this fellow to be so vulgar about the home land was tantamount to treason.

- "Well something needs to be done to restore the old order I suppose. The socialists had their chance and look where that got the country? Loads of lazy students smashing up the place.

People living on benefits. It's all too much; people should know their place and be respectful. Britain was built on a healthy respect for class. You knew your place and that was that. It's something that thankfully people respect in this country; although Gee does have some funny youthful ideas about change, the young always do. He'll grow out of it I'm sure."

- "What?"

John was incensed and horrified. Who was this old relic? Anyone who was anyone in London knew the truth. It was a fact. The rich were selling lies and profiting from the poor. Cameron was a liar. The only people tightening their belts in England were the ordinary taxpayers. John thought it was infuriatingly insane how the very people who had caused financial meltdown were all still living the high life and popping the champagne corks throughout London.

- "You can't think that! The welfare state and NHS are probably the best things England has ever given the world,"

he spluttered,

- "...and social housing? How a country treats its poor is exactly how it should be valued."

William chose his middle finger to push up his spectacles, he delighted in alternating his fingers for such a laborious task. He was ashamed to say that he was taking some delight in watching this buffoon flounder in ludicrous arguments and pointless cliches, and it was no surprise at all that he had chosen to bring up the NHS. What a waste of everyone's time and money that had turned out to be, he thought, why pay to keep the poor alive? Death comes to us all. Essentially the NHS is Aneurin Bevan's vainglorious attempt to delay the inevitable. Pure vanity on his part; but then again nobody is more self righteous than a miner. It was William's opinion that possibly the only good thing that awful Thatcher women had done was bring the miners to order. He hated her with a passion, *jumped up shop girl,* he thought, but she did have gumption.

- "...And so what if I would have England back from the 20th Century?"

He said rather pompously,

- "the few will always have everything at the expense of the many, living here you should know that. Look at that Thaksin fellow, he clearly took a leaf out of Mrs Thatchers book, or perhaps that's just young Gee's influence playing on my mind? Thailand is unashamedly an oligarchy and corrupt and so is England whether you like it or not. It is the way of the world.

The only good thing to come out of socialism was Hitler, and that proved monumentally bad for pretty much everyone, fantastic uniforms though the Nazis, always very presentable..."

By this point John was swaying and even the prospect of more beer could not keep him focused. He had to laugh though, this old man was so off the mark it was ridiculous. *Did he just say something complementary about Hitler?*

Too hot.

Too hot here and, wasn't it Christmas?

John had begun to unravel and he looked out at the grimy Soi with it's massage parlours and go-go bars and found nothing but satisfaction. There had been rain, but it had not washed anything clean, it had tumbled rather pointlessly for an hour and then dried leaving nothing but a pungent stench that tore apart his nostrils like sulphur. It was dirty here and depraved, but John couldn't help thinking that the only thing that separated Silom from Soho was the fallacy of a cold sterile breeze. At least the people who were being fucked here were not having to suffer the indignity of being lied to in the freezing cold.

He breathed in the honesty which was coloured with stagnant fumes and the most beautiful smell of good food.

William was secretly pleased that John was pissed. *Who is the old fool now?* He thought, somewhat maliciously. It surprised him immensely when the glaze lifted from John's eyes and all at once he became lucid again. *You have to admire his pluck* he thought.

- "The 20th century has given us modern democracy, and reason and votes for women and... God! Well, pretty much everything! London has given the world so much!"

He ranted.

- "I love London for all that, and it embarrasses me to see what it's become."
- "Oh really? Do you really believe that? If so then why come to a place which is everything that London pretends it is not?"

One could almost say that William was gloating, there is nothing more unappealing than looking at a grown man delight in the misery of another.

John shook his head and conceded the point. *Why was he here again?* There were shadows dancing on the wall, things that were not real.

- "It's the honesty I suppose; my partner was so pretentious. He wanted to live this whole *gay London life* thing that seemed so false and... Well it was just a load of shit! Wasn't it? It was all about having the latest designer things, and meeting all the family, and to be honest, all the things I wanted to avoid by coming out as a gay man."

William blushed red and instantly felt guilty, he once again shuffled his rotund frame and adjusted the straps of his braces. *Poor fellow,* he thought, *he's here nursing a broken heart.*

- "You shouldn't worry about that too much, with all the freedom that is now afforded to gentlemen of our persuasion in London, there will always be other hurdles. Things rarely ever change significantly. One will always face impediments to enlightened progress. "

Although he was attempting to be kind, he actually came across quite patronizing. "Would you care for another beer?"

Outside the glass fronted bar filled with diplomats and ex-servicemen, the go-go boys and prostitutes were gearing up for another busy night, and they bustled past shrieking lady boys who cackled and adjusted their bras. Neon lights were sparking into action, and John watched with joy as an entire family on a scooter bike laughingly beeped their way through a crowd of gay boys who looked quite bashful. *This whole place is a paradox* he thought to himself. *How do they make it work?*

William was beginning to warm to this John character, it was a feeling close to condescension. An unkind observer might well consider him quite smug. William had his Gee, and all this fellow had was *Chang,* a much less agreeable companion.

"It is remarkable here isn't it." He said, an olive branch that was accepted with the first real smile he had seen John deliver. John fiddled with the base of his frosted glass and smiled to himself.

"I just don't know how they do it? They get everything done and they have so little and still seem so happy." William nodded.

- "Oh I'm sure the climate has something to do with it, that of course and the residual effects of Buddhist philosophy; interesting faith, not confined to ancient texts it somehow seems to breathe. It all seems so much more relevant doesn't it?"

A policeman wearing a pristine mushroom coloured uniform arrived and began chatting with some security guards and prostitutes who were stood opposite. He nonchalantly lit up a cigarette and looking over at the bar in which William and John were sitting, he stood to attention and clicked his heels together offering a courteous nod. John couldn't conceal his surprise and shrugged a smiling guffaw. William graciously returned the nod.

- "He recognizes me from the British club I think. They always look immaculate don't they? Perhaps a little too clean, though he is rather dashing is he not?"

James had previously hated men in uniforms, to him they all looked bland and conventional, but this man was the living embodiment of Bangkok, he was relaxed and louche and yet with a click of his heels he had become rigid, almost statuesque. It all seemed like a perfectly contrived lie.

Through the jumble of street clutter that purveyed every conceivable delicacy on Thanon Silom, a figure emerged, neon lit with gentle grace; a figure who transcended all the shambles of daily life and seemed so calm and beautiful.

A poet.

William blushed a rather boyish scarlet, "ah." He said, composing himself, and once again the perspiration melted down his cheeks. "There's young Gee now."

Through the drunken fog John focused on the approaching man. Gee's eyes were translucent, there was no malice there; he was olive and tan and red reflecting all the colours of the trashy signs that blinked garishly. His red t-shirt looked disheveled and was spattered with yellow paint and it was this uncharacteristic scruffiness that captivated John. He realised this young man was not what he'd expected. The policeman's eyes burned with salutation and he called out, they knew each other, and John assumed they had been lovers.

Why?

John frequently misunderstood the intimacy of Thai body language. It always seemed to him that Thai men where much more comfortable with physical intimacy. In his head, full of Chang as it was, he assumed all men in Thailand were lovers, wishful thinking perhaps. John gradually became aware that he was still sprawled rather slovenly at the bar with William, he felt a little shocked. *Did the old man know his boy was fucking the policeman?*

Gee radiated wholesome affection and there was laughter and John couldn't quite make out what they were saying. It didn't matter anyway, he knew how to ask for a beer in Thai and that was all.

William spoke slowly as if in deep contemplation.

- "His parents are farmers you know, quite well off rural types. People in the provinces are so easy to deceive and yet they give their loyalty so completely. It's something feudal and archaic, for want of a better word I'd say it's *earthy.*"

He had stopped staring at Gee and was looking down at his crumpled shirt, he wondered if he could ever find a laundry that employed the use of starch.

John was engrossed in watching the young willowy Gee smile and be tactile with his policeman friend. They looked so out of place, he thought. *Would you ever see such a display of genuine affection in London?* Friends comfortably stroking each other in public?

Theirs was an old bond forged through joy and pain and it showed. *What about William?* He thought, will he ever have that connection with Gee? Such familiarity? John mulled this thought over in the context of his last relationship and realized that perhaps communication in relationships was the problem. It was only when couples were actually forced to speak to each other about everything in their lives that things started to go wrong. Perhaps the old man had the right idea, there is a place for silence.

"Yes 'earthy'." Continued William, this time he had removed his annoying spectacles and was feverishly rubbing away the condensation with a cloth napkin.

- "They're not disconnected from the land you see, they place their lives in the here and now and not in the vague hope of something better. Theirs is the promise of the here and now."

John watched as Gee parted from his policeman friend and inside him something broke, some vague recollection of intimacy that he had forgotten. Something in him snapped.

William once more adjusted his spectacles, this time using three of his fingers, and he meticulously placed them over his bulbous nose. For John this whole scenario had taken a ridiculous turn and he wondered for a moment if perhaps another Chang beer was a good idea.

Gee motioned in and looked for William. Their eyes were locked as Gee drifted towards the bar and a smile erupted over his beautifully sculpted face. William was composed but elated and it was apparent he could not contain his excitement.

- "I love him you see and I believe that he loves me too, old fool that I am. Sometimes One should forget what is rational and allow oneself the indulgence to just believe."

It was at that precise moment that John made up his mind to stay here forever.

"Even the unlovable can find love," he mumbled randomly and then for the first time in years he was profoundly lost for words.

# PART 4 - SATHON - NOVEMBER - 2010

Horst Weihnachten was never known for being liberal with his cash. In fact he was known, back in Hamburg, for being something of a miser. Despite owning numerous *wohnung* and apartment blocks, he would drive a Volkswagen Polo and wear a cheap, unbranded shell-suit. However; here in Thailand, he relaxed his purse strings and his rather bulging belt and indulged himself in all the most frivolous boys that Bangkok could offer.

He was a peculiar contradiction of eccentricities that confounded the innocent onlooker, and he forever kept his friends on their toes. He was Polish, born in Russia to a family of old German money. In certain company he would make reference to his Jewish roots, but he was cautious of this. How such an obscure lineage could be cultivated by just two parents was a constant mystery to all, although it remained a fact that Horst would rarely ever expand upon the question of his heritage. Such bizarre inconsistency was only highlighted by the fact that Horst appeared so warm and loving. His red cheeks welcomed you warmly and on meeting him, you could easily mistake him for a harmless old fool. That impression would leave very quickly. Old friends and new seemed to embrace his meanness. They lived with the fact that here was a man who would spend thousands of Euro's a night on boys and booze; yet, he would be the first man knocking on your door asking for the return of the 100 baht that he had lent you in a drunken moment of madness the night before.

He chose to stay at *"The Malaya Hotel,"* for several reasons. Firstly, it was within convenient taxi distance of the notorious nightlife, massage parlours, bordellos and sex shows in '*Boyztown*' in Surawong.

Secondly, the rooms were spacious and practical, not too spartan, but not too opulent. It was by Bangkok standards incredibly cheap, a fact which had not eluded him. The main reason he liked to frequent the Malaya, was their ability to respect his particular indulgences and never question him about his rather dubious guests. Most of his boys he found in the cafe of the hotel, or lounging by the pool. There they languished under the misapprehension that a night with Horst could lead to a whole new life, occasionally he found boys online, but they were frequently unreliable and hugely problematic with regards to drink and drugs.

Horst had been accompanied to Bangkok on this particular occasion by one of his oldest friends and companions Peter.

Peter was a gentleman in his 80's and like Horst he had been a notorious homosexual in German society for many years; however, they were different in so many ways. Peter was affluent but not wealthy, and he saw money as something to be enjoyed and not hoarded. Peter had had the experience of loving relationships and had always relished the companionship of a partner in his life.

They had both been handsome in their youth. They had enjoyed the attentions that such gifts had brought, but Horst had once had it all; money and beauty and a standing in German society that had amounted to fame. So now, in his later years, he had become quite jealous. He hated the fact that he had grown old. It all seemed so unfair.

Fate was cruel, it had given him everything, and though he still had the money, life now felt somehow empty and pointless. He had slowly but surely seen everything slip away, and the excitement he incited upon entering a room had fizzled to a cynical widening of the prostitutes eyes as they measured his worth. He constantly berated Peter for not scrimping and saving and not being more proactive in making money. To the outsider, he could seem rather cruel, but he was actually being quite compassionate, in his mind he was his brother's keeper.

Peter had loved and he had lost and secretly he pitied his friend.

They had been planning their winter vacation for some time, and Peter had invited his young second cousin Bryan along. Bryan had come out as gay and was living and working in Frankfurt. *How things had changed* Peter thought, the young boys today could be so flippant and free and so open! But then, thinking about it, so had he all those years ago. *Was he ever so young and so reckless*? He must have been; but then, sexual indiscretions have always been the privilege of those who can afford to keep the silence.

They had booked three adjacent rooms at Horst's request and Peter had known instantly that this was for many reasons, none of which were compassionate or adult. Peter knew that it would entertain Horst immensely to meddle in the affairs of the young Bryan. He would view the boy through envious eyes and manipulate and venomously toy with him. Spite would be Horst's primary motivation, as much as Peter loved his old friend dearly, he knew he would be forced to placate and mediate. Even though they had never been introduced, Peter knew that Horst was jealous of Bryan. For Bryan was young and reckless and full of the confidence that life imbues, he was on an adventure.

Peter had loved and lost and had ingratiated himself with the fact that his life had been lived to the full. It truly broke his aging heart to see his friend ravaged by so much unrest. Horst would buy the prettiest boys and take them to his rooms just to elicit some form of envy from his friends. Peter knew that, beyond the merriment, Horst felt somewhat betrayed by life and behind every complicit smile there remained a darker cloud of resentment. Horst's motivations towards Bryan were fuelled by the remnants of a faded vanity.

As much as Horst loved all the distractions of Bangkok, he loathed the city itself. For him it was dirty and it seemed there was no rationale to the madness. Exquisite modernity flourished amid the medieval chaos and the contradictions were all too much for him. Everywhere it seemed the feral soi-dogs would drag their pitiful bones around the clutter.

There were too many feral dogs in Bangkok for Horst; they were an uncomfortable reminder of a sorry past; refugee bitches that scurried from owner to owner. They were scraggy-haired, rabid beasts that looked unclean and riddled with syphilitic madness.

In Europe the dogs were now mostly placid, they were docile and temperate and apart from the occasional barks of dissatisfaction, they were really quite tame. They sat in cosy rooms and were distracted by meaningless entertainments. This suited Horst. He could finally see some order to the madness and the rabid dogs were something of a distant memory. Perhaps that is why he came to Bangkok to play amongst the feral hounds, secretly he needed to know that they were still alive somewhere in the world. They were still shambling around making a mockery of human progress. They were the constant reminder of something simmering just beneath the surface, prisoners in a cave seeing only the shadows on the wall.

They were un-neutered and directionless:

They were slavering and vicious, a living testament to all that Horst thought was base.

Peter enjoyed the fact that he was now a happy old dog with no new tricks to learn, when he looked at Bryan, he could see something quite beautiful. He believed that things were getting better.

Bryan saw nothing but filth in Bangkok, he embraced all that was modern and he disliked everything that was unclean. He didn't see the stray dogs ambling around the streets, *why should he*? He was on holiday and a taxi could take him from one cabaret to the next, no need to bother with all that filth and misery.

But the dogs were here in the open, not pedigreed and pampered like in Europe; they ambled on the pavements outside the hotels frequented by tourists. They scavenged for scraps and behind their dark, dark eyes there was the madness. They displayed none of the polite affectations that Europeans had attributed them and they were loyal to no one. They were flea-bitten and ragged and they haunted Horst's periphery, playing on his mind all the time. Here in Bangkok they walked the streets at night.

. . . . . . . . . . . . .

Bryan had met an Englishman and was causing a stir amongst the German friends. They had been inseparable and were out exploring Thailand with a fascination that only the young at heart can ever muster.

An Englishman?

*How very modern.*

Horst had taken an instant dislike to the Englishman, on account of him being English, and he had taken much pleasure ridiculing their friendship. Every morning at breakfast Horst would insinuate that the Englishman was lying about his age, *he clearly wasn't 37!* He was born with one of those faces that seemed younger, even though he was much older. Peter naturally placated his old friend as the conversations got out of hand and Bryan became more and more agitated.

Maybe it was the heat that irritated Horst? Maybe it was the Englishman? Secretly what plagued him the most was the way the Englishman strode among the beastly hounds and gloated at their savagery. He seemed, to Horst, to be so self-righteous. He would walk among them without a care and appeared to be impervious to their deathly stares. It was almost as if he believed that he was not the object of their conscious glowering. Surely all the spectral hounds should haunt the Englishmen as much as any other European? To walk among the soi-dogs and feel no shame, he was clearly raised a liar. *He was never 37.*

. . . . . . . . . . . . .

And so it came to a late supper one evening in the courtyard cafe of the hotel, Horst and Peter were sipping a relaxing nightcap. Horst's was pink and contained champagne and the glass was decadently vulgar, something modelled on a classical figure. Peter sipped Cognac. Both were silently awaiting the arrival of their absent young friend.

Gruffly, Horst studied the fresh selection of boys who had arrived for the evening. They were all too pretty and full of false smiles, far too feral and tired; he could smell their desperation and that was instantly off putting. The boys were fresh from the north and keen to make a living. Tonight he fancied entertainment not business, and in the distance he winced at the sight of panting tan dogs circling, *there must be thousands out there* he thought.

Peter sipped calmly and listened to the music of water trickling into a pond, in Europe it snowed, how lucky he was to be sitting sipping cognac, an old man warm and content.

The table next to them was occupied by an American, an African American to be precise, from near Chicago. He was hefty and worked for the government and he carried himself with a dignity that so few people dare. Large and solid he sat smiling. He was entertaining a sprightly young Cambodian chap whose eyes glistened. Together they drank sweet Thai whisky and talked pidgin English about their home countries. Occasionally their eyes betrayed the contract that bound them, only occasionally, this is Bangkok.

Midnight and the mosquito's were nipping, a taxi pulled up and out bundled young Bryan and his English friend. They were embarrassingly drunk, and seemed shockingly out of place amid the silent bartering of the courtyard cafe crowd.

They stepped, giggling and chuckling, over some dozy soi-dogs who scratched lazily at the biting fleas. Naturally, Horst was impeccably charming and spoke English to welcome their guests. He hated speaking English, but he knew how much it flattered them that their mongrel tongue had become universal. "Hello boys! How are you? I do hope you have enjoyed your evening's entertainments, please join us, sit." He motioned to the waitress to bring more chairs.

On hearing English, the American gentleman became momentarily distracted from his young companion and responded by turning his chair and politely said, "Hey how's it going?" "Very well indeed!" smiled Horst; for the cocktail had made him lucid and tonight he would be charm incarnate.

Bryan and his English companion were speaking German; every time the Englishman spoke Horst winced; he managed to make the language obscenely camp. *How he mutilates the mother tongue.* They laughed at the recounting of one of their earlier adventures. Upon meeting Horst for the first time, the Englishman had extended his hand warmly and in perfect German introduced himself. They shook hands and what really upset Horst was that the Englishman bowed slightly when he had politely introduced himself to Peter. He had been like a young suitor addressing the father of his betrothed. Horst was infuriated but masked it well. They had obviously been talking and Bryan had expressed his preference for Peter. *This Englishman couldn't be 37.* His hair was greying but he did have a fresh face - was it surgery? Was he just blessed with a charming appearance and a youthful countenance? Horst made a note to bring up the subject of payment at breakfast tomorrow. Bryan was in his late 20's and shouldn't be whoring his arse to an old Englishman for nothing.

"How do you do?" inquired the Englishman of the American, *so affected,* thought Horst. Only common people would ever be so affected. English people who have money speak so badly and dress so shabbily; this man was impeccably attired, he positively reeked of humble beginnings. He was clearly bright too; which was dull, anyone who is anyone in English society is generally a complete moron. They are a nation of inconsistencies.

In the car-park the scabby soi-dogs stirred.

"Hey I'm fine, it's a beautiful evening, you been in Bangkok long?" beamed the American, and Horst managed to conceal his disdain with the utmost charm. It had not escaped his attention that in the presence of the Englishman, the American had neglected to introduce his Cambodian companion; an act of guilt perhaps? Horst had discovered a certain poison in the moment which had appealed to his broken sense of balance. *Sickening,* thought Horst, it was like watching an old slave seeking affirmation from an old master. This infuriated him and he put his had to his chest to steady his heart. The Cambodian boy was beautiful and over 18, though he looked much younger, and Horst wanted the man to brag of his conquest. This Englishman was nothing, he was nobody, how dare the man feel ashamed. The Englishman continued to chatter completely oblivious to this.

"We've had the most wonderful day, we went to a temple and then ended up at a show in *Phat-Pong!* It was incredibly decadent," he chirped.

"The cabaret was hilarious and the boys all had the most enormous dicks," laughed Bryan with the thickest German clip. "Was it at Slippy-queens?" asked Horst. "Yes, Slippy-queens," said Bryan, rather curtly; his puppy-dog eyes twinkled with whiskey and concentration as he played with the foreign language. "Oh Slippy-queens is such fun," gushed Horst, "I do hope you sent my regards to the owner Daniel," Bryan hesitated, was it because he was having trouble formulating his English? "Yes, he urgh - sent, yes, sent over a bottle of whiskey..."

"Daniel is such a dear, he has some of the finest young boys in Bangkok and they are always so, how do you say, accommodating?" The Englishman roared with laughter at Horst's double entendre. "Indeed they were, Bryan and I had the rather expensive pleasure of having them talk at our table, I say '*expensive,*' but really it was only a few thousand Baht which is nothing, I can see why so many westerners get lost here..." As the Englishman said this, Horst noticed the American duck his head - one might be tempted to call it a wince.

The Cambodian remained graciously ignored and the chatter around the table rose and became more animated as Bryan and his friend delighted the guests with anecdotes of their evening of sex-shows and man-whores.

The mosquito's were small and fast and nipped at exposed ankles and out in the darkness, across the car-park, by the waiting motorbike taxis, the soi-dogs were troubled by something approaching. Instinctively they dragged their mongrel carcasses to attention and ears raised they dispersed with sullen yelps and lazy barks; something visceral and dangerous approached. The instinct to survive was paramount, even in those mangy old bones, and they evaporated into the night to cower. They looked on at the approaching madness through sorry eyes.

The movement of the dogs had not gone unnoticed by Horst who smiled and allowed himself the indulgence of languishing in the pleasant conversation. Even though he thought the Englishman unsuitably common, he felt a sense of calm. *This is how things should be*, he thought, old men sitting at a table drinking, being entertained by everyone else.

"...and so I paid him 500 baht and he just sat there wanking his cock..." said Bryan, his English improving with every swig of sweet Thai whiskey and coke.

In a gluttonous moment of indulgence Horst imagined the two of them fucking. They were handsome and they were clearly enjoying each others bodies. At times he would catch glances and contact between them that betrayed a certain tenderness. It was something almost wholesome and untainted by money and age. Wholesome? Here? At *'The Malaya Hotel?'* At a table where even the sanctimonious American had avoided inviting God into the conversation. This is not the city for tenderness. How he envied them, in his heart he wished for nothing but a wailing sadness to descend upon their smiles and bring them sorrow. He calmed himself with the knowledge that this was merely a holiday romance. He took comfort from knowing that they would soon be left slightly older, with nothing to show for this moment but a fading memory.

The Thai men who rode the motorbike taxis had left their contented conversation and were all stood meowing tonal sounds and pointing at something in the dark. Where they drunk? *How typically irresponsible*, thought Horst as he finished his drink and motioned for the waiter.

- "I hate the dogs here, look at that one,"

gestured the kindly faced American, his eyes wide and slightly bloodshot.

Travelling at some pace across the carpark towards the cafe lurched a cumbersome bitch. She had white and brown patches that disguised her angry sores. Even at a distance, her one blind eye was noticeable, it seemed unfocused as it searched and it searched and it seemed to rest upon the gathering of westerners. She breathed heavily and panted, shaking her head from side to side. Matted, white drool hung around her jowls - she flashed from left to right biting at the night and growling. She lashed out at something that plagued her but it was an unfocused strike. There were too many distractions and she stopped for a second, seemingly to defend herself from an unseen attacker. It was a red shadow that surrounded her, it crept inwards and she could feel it all around her and it constricted her every fibre. She was bound to something unseen and it dried her throat and made her thirsty for revenge. She was completely powerless to the thing that controlled her, in her mind it was everywhere.

Her presence had elicited something resembling a panic in the local Thai people that the western guests had hitherto unseen, and it was this that alerted them to the danger. The conversation halted and the American stood and motioned to the waiter who was barking orders at a worried looking waitress.

- "You got yourself a rabid dog here!"

He shouted, he was gesticulating urgently and seemed completely oblivious to the fact that his instructions went unheeded,

- "you have to move these people!"

The Germans and the Englishman watched in silence, but appeared nonchalant; they had the air of having seen this drama played out before, and resigned themselves to the fact that this story would unfold as it should. The Englishman calmly took a sip of whiskey and lit Bryan's cigarette. "Shall we go to the river tomorrow?" He asked of his new lover, "I've heard a boat-trip here is to die for..." He stroked Bryan's arm and Peter nodded calmly and smiled to himself.

Horst was agitated that he had finished his drink, and he could not understand what all the fuss was about, *where was that confounded waiter*? He was thirsty and the sentimentality of the Englishman was intolerable.

The hound was gripped with fury and rattled out a rasping bark that grated in the air.

RED!

RED! RED!

She snapped at all the unseen ghosts and every turn she took betrayed an angry stance. She danced alone against the threat of darkness, and her jaws ached from snatching at her foe. Her silver eye could not fix upon a target and even with it closed she could not make out her enemy. There were too many distractions.

A policeman on a motorbike arrived and within seconds all the Thai people were placated; for them the panic was over. All of a sudden, completely unspoken, a sense of temporary capitulation settled over the grounds of the hotel.

The waiter asked the guests politely and calmly to move inside to the restaurant. Horst seized this opportunity to request another drink and Bryan and the Englishman asked if they could smoke inside.

The American was frantically drilling the other guests with incomprehensible instructions; they all smiled and complied, though it was obvious that none of them understood a word he was saying. He seemed convinced of his own ability to lead, but to everyone else he looked ridiculous. The Cambodian boy hid a smile behind his hands; *poor boy,* thought Horst, he knew that later the boy would bear the brunt of all the pumped up bravado.

Horst looked out through the glass window into the car-park. The policeman gestured and he was obeyed by the people who moved silently. Quietly Horst observed that there was some method to the madness here. He witnessed the rabid bitch fall and he lowered his eyes at the old sound of gunshot as it echoed around the courtyard. He hated that sound more than anything.

Peter, who had been having trouble moving his old bones, finally came to rest in a comfortable chair and was now intent on settling here for the evening. All this moving around at his age wasn't good for him. The sound of gunshot was something to which he would never grow accustomed, yet it had always offered a solution.

- "And that is how you deal with that,"

he said thoughtfully, and looking mournfully into his glass for just a second he took a long sip of Cognac.

"Indeed it is sir," echoed the Englishman, "indeed it is..."

# PART 3 - SOHO - OCTOBER - 2010

Nights when company eludes me, I grab a *'Private eye'* and head here to "Balans," on "Old Compton street."

I treat myself to breakfast and beer, and I watch the heady dramas unfold.

As much as I love Soho, any Londoner will tell you, it has an underside that is lamentable. Its history is held within the hunting call of its name. Now the hunters have become the hunted and the internet has rendered many of the sleazy drinking holes in Soho obsolete. It has become a sanitised version of itself.

I remember as a young man seeing hope in every bulb on every Billboard. Furthermore, I found the darker side exhilarating. The narrative of sleaze is so appealing to provincial men like me. People who see fun in everything are drawn here. People who were allowed to be naive, once upon a time, was I ever that naive?

I'm sure that's what drew Michael Carmichael here too, for he was a young pioneer. No doubt about it.

Was it really ten years ago that I had met him?

Yes it was.

Almost a decade had passed and here he is, exactly where I had met him.

Michael Carmichael is sitting at the next table and so far he has not recognised me.

He looks good. He is very smart. Stubble grazes his chin, and it leads the eye quite naturally down the line of his neck to his unbuttoned, tie-less shirt. He has, apparently, at last come to terms with his money. He is at ease displaying the trappings of his affluent life. Previously he had taken great pains to disguise his wealth.

We were so much younger then.

This is Soho, London. A place that is the living embodiment of so many stories, of all the people, who have ever travelled through its streets. Indeed, it is a place everyone should experience at least once in their life. It remains the reason why I ran away from the still, dark, country nights.

From what I can remember, Michael Carmichael relished the opportunity to reference the fact that he is Irish. Every nuance of his character is attributed to this heritage. He particularly likes to link it to any imagined indiscretion or insignificant misdemeanor - he has too much to drink, it's down to his genes. He slurs his words, well, what do you expect? It was almost immediately apparent that he was American.

We have Irish people here, and some of them have even been to Ireland. He described himself as;

- "Fifth generation Irish, and Jewish on my mothers side!"

Which, I remember thinking, could refer to anyone from north London; also, it technically made him Jewish. It was a confusing narrative, I thought to myself, yet typically American.

He suited this part of town. Soho, like America, is a mix of mythology and style. So many people claim it is their home and paint it with their stories, it wears so many different colours.

Ten years have passed:

A decade:

He was so much younger then, and yet he hasn't aged a bit. Seeing him here has suddenly made me feel so much older. Perhaps I am too old, that is why he no longer recognises me.

To be honest he hadn't really grabbed my attention, back then, as much as the old soak he was with.

He had been joined by an older gentleman, who had decided to wear a mannequin from the window of, *"Lipman and Sons."* He perfectly embodied every cliché of an aging old theatrical lovey. The man was a living parody. He wore a cravat, a brimmed hat, and layers of old vintage tat that conspired to render him quite foolish. He had dyed his hair, cultivating a greasy brown effect, so it shone unnaturally chestnut around his pursed, wrinkled face. One might assume that he was channeling Quentin Crisp rather poorly, which really isn't a good thing.

Young Mr Carmichael was engrossed in, what appeared to be, a colourful conversation with the old soak. The old chap was, in true London fashion, embellishing his monologues with anecdotes that reeked of implausible situations and improbable time-lines. I remember feeling rather embarrassed as the young Michael Carmichael appeared to wallow in the tall tales. He lapped up the fantasy that here, in bohemian Europe, he had stumbled upon the only true eccentric aristocrat left in Soho. The old queen rambled on...

- "Of course, you see, we used to have our own box-wallah in the house, whose Aunt made the most delectable curried mullet. Not a patch, I suppose, on your own native catfish but still, never the less, the perfect accompaniment to stimulating provincial conversation. As a young and handsome American, you must be absolutely infuriated by the sheer weight of trivial mumblings given credence by your parochial brethren?"

"Oh my God it all sounds so cool," said the young man excitedly, "I've never been to India, I've heard it's amazing. I'm hoping to get there after I've checked out Europe!"

- "... Oh my dear boy! I shouldn't bother going there now! These days it's full of Indians! It's frightfully barbaric, not a soul living there worth mentioning..."

To the unseasoned Londoner this would all sound impressively authentic, but I noted the fraying on his jacket and his slacks. He had a thousand yard stare and his portentous turn of phrase betrayed his humble English roots. Nobody in Soho, in *"Balans,"* so early in the morning could possibly be *old money.*

Or was he? For a moment I doubted my own conviction. However, that quickly passed as I heard the old love continue his yarn.

- "...I first toured India with the army you know, dear boy. The girls were coy and the boys furnished me with every indulgent vice a young officer could wish for! They're a confusing mass of contradictions, the Indians, the only reliable thing one can say about the Indians, is they are inherently unreliable..."

This never happened, I remember thinking to myself. I had grown up in a Navy family. I was used to the exaggerated yarns of adventure, I knew all the signs of artifice. These are the tales that are spun in order to cease the grating pain of truth, and I remember being intrigued as to what the pain might be.

- "I am Stanley Montgomery Smithe, of the Southampton Smithes; a pleasure to make your acquaintance."

This was the clincher. As soon as he said that I knew that he was full of shit.

He was a complete fantasist. Maybe he was from Southampton, but really - "*Smithe?*"

All at once I saw through to the root of this performance. Stan Smith had probably left Southampton in search of a theatrical career. A move which had subsequently led to a string of jobs in the service industry. This had probably fuelled his warped sense of entitlement, hence the affected accent, and the stories? Well, they were the kind of stories that anyone has heard and many have shared over bars or at boozy tables. London is awash with implausible tales. Judging by Stanley's scarily, staring eyes, he had probably learned quite quickly from therapy groups at AA or rehab; nobody is willing to dish the dirt more than those seeking forgiveness. It was clear to anyone that Stanley's vice of choice was booze. I think this was his enabler. I had visions of him attending AA meetings swearing repentance, and greedily consuming the narratives of those more suited to the luxury of talking their way through life. I'm pretty sure he had peddled the lives of others in order to appear infinitely more worldly wise.

Yes; in many ways the party had finished for Stanley Smith, but in one last ditched attempt to make a play for greatness, he had fashioned the ultimate London caricature. It was a creature of pure affected artifice; a magnanimous invention of parody, "*Stanley Montgomery Smithe,*" was never born - he was created. He had taken to the tables of Soho entertaining tourists and giving them the anecdotes they required. He had fashioned a life here and, even though he was completely artificial, he somehow perfectly encapsulated an authentic vision of Soho.

I was hooked.

I was more than prepared to step outside my comfort zone and breach my self imposed barrier of insecurities just to hear this story. I decided to throw caution to the wind and ingratiate myself with the young tourist Mr Carmichael. However, I really wanted to make a night of getting to know the truth behind the mysterious Mr Smithe.

Fortunately Mr Smithe - whoever he is - took his scarlet stained lips to the toilet just as Michael's food arrived; a move, no doubt, cultivated to conceal his own hunger.

I started talking to Michael Carmichael.

- "That's quite a character you've found there, or did he find you? Either way, you do realise he's mental don't you?"

He looked at me and delighted me with a chuckle that displayed the cutest dimple and of course impeccable teeth.

- "He suits the place very well, and to think I was told that Londoners never spoke to strangers. So far I've been approached by two. I take it you're from here?"

A dig at me perhaps? So many people can be sensitive about their roots, and having lived in London for years and been subjected to the endless rounds of, "*what's your name and where you from?*" conversations, I must admit, I was always a little weary of revealing where I was from. Michael wasn't like that though, he seemed perfectly interested and so I was beginning to find him all the more attractive. Once again my own insecurities crept up on me. I had found that I could no longer talk to people that I found attractive. Having worked in the entertainment industry for many years I had grown accustomed to criticism, I was instinctively waiting for the bitchy comment that never came, yet still I concealed my own heritage and swiftly changed the subject.

- "He's great isn't he, a proper old character, only in Soho right? So, do you mind if I join you and find out the story?"
- "Of course! Shit I'm up for that..."

On returning from the bathroom Stanley made some small talk and eyed me with suspicion. I decided to work hard to wheedle my way in and win his affection, even though it was clear the object of his affection was Michael. I could sense that he was used to dealing with tourists and he could see that I had him pegged as a fraud. However, in front of the American, he decided to be courteous and welcoming.

- "You must excuse me boys, I appear to have left my wallet in my rooms on Charing Cross road, if I could trouble you for the bill I can invite you both for a night-cap there... It is a much more private space, more conducive to our purpose of enlightened conversation..."

I was taken aback by this, for just a moment. Could he be the genuine article? A bonafide eccentric millionaire? I mean seriously, who has rooms on Charing Cross anymore?

As people do in such situations, I had quickly established a warm camaraderie with the young Michael Carmichael, we were like young boys on an adventure. It struck me as endearing just how quickly bonds can be formed between strangers. Yes, I felt we understood each other, and the trust was forthcoming. In just a few short minutes I knew I was safe with him. I have always sought comfort in the glint of a smiling eye, even though that course of action has frequently proved treacherous (and yes I have the tattoo to prove it), but I wouldn't have it any other way. Life is about trusting people, and in London, I had forgotten that.

We paid our bill for our food, and Stanley's bottle(s) of red-wine, (he was there for under an hour) then we made our way out into the chill of Old Compton street, the swinging heart of gay London, or is it? Gay Soho just seemed like it was going through the motions, it no longer excited me anymore.

*What is it with gay men and really shit music?* I thought to myself as we followed Mr Smithe towards Charring Cross road. *Handbag house* of the most mediocre shitness echoed out from all of the pubs and the bars. I can't help feeling it's the kind of music that is made solely for the purpose of sodomising strangers and imbibing bucket loads of cheap poppers, which isn't a bad thing I suppose, but it's not really conducive to anything else. It could be worse, it could be white boys doing Gangster rap, and there's never going to be any excuse for that.

Is this what has become of the rave generation?

Jeremy Joseph and G.A.Y.

I can't help thinking to myself, *these people do realise that this is really shit house music don't they?*

As far as house music goes, "hand-bag," or "funky house," is the fag end of lazy creativity. Furthermore, it constantly amazes me that ten years have passed and the same music plays on the same relentless, turgid beat. A beat that once seemed quite exciting for a while:

*"The great dance music revolution!"*

What a joke that was, and we were all such willing dupes. I seem to remember that once, back in the 90's, I believed that the revolution could be started on the dance floor, just like every other wishful thinking loon, what on earth was I thinking? Just like any other scene it had it's day. Yet still this soulless repetitive music is produced. It is a constant reminder to me that pop has eaten itself.

Maybe I'm wrong. Perhaps I got old and the world of music moved on without me; so, what's the point in criticising something I no longer care about?

We crossed the road at rickshaw junction and followed Stan to a door just opposite from "*Les Miserables.*" "Les mis," is a misery memoir turned into liquid gold by happy show-folk. I kid you not, it's a musical about the French revolution. Who'd have thought misery could be so much fun? What next? A musical about the holocaust? I'm sure not even Dame Andrew Lloyd Webber herself could make Bergen-Belsen and jazz-hands go together. Scratch that, I suppose it worked for Liza's "*Cabaret,*" oh good grief, it would appear that in the world of showbiz we can make a song and dance about anything.

Charring Cross road I love you.

Michael had taken the lead in engaging Stanley in small talk. I couldn't help thinking that this had put Stanley at ease. He was still a little suspicious of my motives; however, my motives were not to bed Michael or indeed bed Mr Smithe, I was simply curious. My motives were much more figurative. I was being a voyeur. Indeed, being a voyeur is conducive with the life here in Soho, visceral action is never really on the table. Unlike other central city seedy sex areas, the sex here is just for show, it's a tourist attraction. The majority of the real action takes place elsewhere.

It was a council flat.

The whole building was council flats. Who has a council flat on

Charing cross road? How amazing is that? Lucky bastard, I thought. Some of the flats were owned by flashy jean wearing media types, who obviously detested the council tenants, but the majority of flats where still council. It was, as I had thought, all part of Stanley Smiths elaborate fiction. I had decided to play along with "Mr Smithes" fables, he was, if nothing else, an entertaining host.

- "What an amazing flat, this must have cost you a fortune!"

I feigned my naivety well, in so doing I had allowed Mr Smith full license to embellish his environment.

- "It was left to me by my poor dear Mamaaah. She used to tread the boards for her own amusement, oh, if these walls could talk! The people who have been through these doors and graced these halls, such talent, one can only ever feel inadequate in their presence. Mamaaaah would entertain the great actors of her day here you know. I have it on good authority that Noel Coward himself sang in this room and got locked in the lavatory with a young stoker from the coast of Singapore... Heady days..."

The flat was a curious example of madness. It was like a trendy east-London boutique had been detonated in a theatrical dressing room. Despite it's chaos, the room had managed to maintain some sense of order. It was balancing on that fine line between being charmingly eclectic and bat shit insane. The front-room was spacious and exuded dust and by-gone memorabilia. I am guessing it is a true window into the mind of Stanley Smith. It was all at once fascinating and confusing.

Black and white pictures of people who were beautiful and long dead peered out through sequined costumes that were the stuff of pantomimes. It was all eerily coherent.

Stanley Montgomery Smithe poured three large, cheap whiskeys without ice and proceeded to put on some Rachmaninoff quietly in the background. It scratched its way through the speakers of a second hand record player and the effect was unsettling to say the least. I imagine this is the sort of place where all bad show-folk go to die.

Michael was flushed, as was I, yet he had managed to guide the now totally inebriated Stanley through an anecdotal minefield. Occasionally, Michael would look over at me and gurn a silent, "*Oh My God,*" or smile. It was a smile of innocence and inhibition. It was a smile that strengthened the bond between us.

- "..You're travelling around Europe you say?"

Continued the Smithe, he was beginning to repeat himself.

- "Ah yes, it's so agreeable here of course I found the Americas so perplexing. One couldn't tell if one was to be shot at or shagged by some of the chaps there, rugged beasts that they are, born of manual labour and cheap meat..."

It was relentless and ridiculous.

He flitted from one country or era to the next without stopping for breath. It had rapidly become a recital of empty words and pointless stories, one look around this room was enough to convince anyone that it was clear that this man had not left the flat in decades. He was a traveller of the mind. As to the mans age, well, it was like the decoration of the flat, completely indeterminable.

Michael Carmichael sat and clearly relished these stories, what were his intentions? He was clearly well versed in the language of concealment, I couldn't quite figure him out at all. He couldn't possibly have been contemplating sleeping with Stan could he? I honestly had no idea that he had been interested in me.

I had been quite full of booze, and I remember being aware that Michael had become more attractive with every swig of wretchingly awful whiskey. I was studying him with ever an increasing intensity, the back of his neck, his face. I traced the line from his crown to his shoulders. To stop myself from staring in a boozy, stalker fashion, I averted my gaze and continued to look around the musty old room.

Pictures and posters were everywhere. They alluded to nostalgic decadence and, as I had assumed, an obsession with the Theatre. Such madness!

Why do people acquaint something as silly as acting and singing with fame, celebrity and greatness? Is this the same in any other industry? Do you have award ceremonies for nurses? Maybe you should!

"...and caffita of the year goes to..."

This obsession with fame had clearly driven Stanley mad, yet still he talked.

- "... and suddenly, of course, I was balls deep in the bursar..."

It had come to my attention that I had said very little, I had nodded my way through most of the early morning chat. When Stanley retired to his kitchen, to fix yet another round of cheap whiskey, I looked over at Michael Carmichael who was perched on a rather shabby, threadbare chaise-lounge. I will carry that picture with me for the rest of my life. His eyes were watery but sharp, not dulled by the drink, they were enlivened, and he appeared to spring into life from the collapsed tatter of a worn out old chair.

"You're totally right, this guy is fucking mental!" He said, "I'm pretty much done here, you want to go grab a beer at my Hotel?"

Our bond of camaraderie had been re-established. He seemed to react to my smile, sometimes it can be the tenderest thing imaginable just to be studied by someone who cares.

- "It's nothing like that, I mean, I'm not hitting on you or anything. I'm not gay. It would be great to talk, I'm kinda new here in town, and I don't know that many people."

I was flustered again, he had made me want him, and now I felt quite ashamed. I thought that I had betrayed our adventure. Had he seen me staring?

Stanley re-entered the room with more drinks and continued as before. Something about, "*serving in Korea*," and, "*employing the services of a Malaysian rent-boy.*" Michael feigned interest and with impeccable politeness, he lied his apologies for leaving. He said he, *"had a plane to catch."* I followed suit and invented a shift at work in the morning. Such rituals are accepted by all but the loneliest of drunks. I recall the pleadings of Stanley Smith with some distaste, vowing never to end up like that Man; so abandoned and so lonely, right here in the heart of Soho.

We left the flat with a stiffled giggle and headed back into the charged up crowds of Charring Cross road. All of a sudden, even though we had only just left him, Stanley Smith had become a thing of the past and there; in my mind, he was not out of place.

He was a character in our shared experience, left far behind, he inhabited the night before and we were hungry for a new adventure. I remember I laughed on a night bus, along with other drunken smiles, then I remember a hotel...

The memory of Michael Carmichael dissolves into visceral sensations.

There, without shame, we had welcomed the morning sunshine in with sex. I remember a feeling of being totally requited, yet somehow completely misunderstood. Or was that somewhere else?

There was a tender inquisitiveness to that morning, it re-invigorated my quest for exploration. Perhaps there really was form to the shadows after all.

I remember the laughter.

I remember Stanley Smith.

. . . . . . . . . . . . . . .

Such characters are the fabric of Soho, though he lived a life of illusion, Stanley Smith has often popped into my mind. I wonder if he is still out there, in some random restaurant or bar, punting out his tales of grandeur. Is he still so desperate for company? Would he still be the old eccentric aristocrat, "*Stanley Montgomery Smithe of the Southampton Smithes?*" Or would he be just plain old Stan Smith? Curiously enough, I hope he is still living the fiction. It suits him, as much as Soho suits my memories of London.

That was all ten years ago.

Stanley Smith is a memory.

He is an indulgence brought on by my sentimental mood. It is inspired by this place. It is inspired by the presence of Michael Carmichael...

Michael Carmichael is sitting at the table next to me and still he hasn't noticed me. He is handsome and is engrossed in a cheeky conversation with his guest. His guest is a particularly sparkly young man, who seems awkward and out of place; he looks new in town. He exudes the undeniable thirst for adventure. Perhaps they are both on an adventure.

I hope so.

I am overwhelmed with the desire to break out and find something new. I am tired of the old stories of Soho. I have become bored of the place that once upon a time I had loved with wide-eyed desire. As I contemplate the many tales and stories of Stan Smith; I envisage the layer upon layer of lives lived in Soho. Every moment is fleeting, the past remains passed in the present.

This place is now part of my history and it is time for me leave.

At this exact moment, I happen to overhear Michael Carmichael lean in towards his new friend and say with genuine camaraderie,

- "You want to go and grab a beer at my hotel? I mean, I'm not hitting on you or anything. I'm not gay. It's just that I'm new here and well, I mean, I don't really know that many people, it would be great to talk..."

# PART 2 – CLAPHAM – SEPTEMBER – 2010

London is a place for the young I think to myself. Youth without wealth can almost always triumph here. The older generations need money In abundance. Gentlemen of a certain age might indulge in hair-plugs and wigs, and older women may well invest their millions extinguishing their wrinkles and greys in the hope of extending their bloom. As we get older our everyday maintenance becomes ever more elaborate.

London is a city constantly striving for the elixir of youth; there is always something new that promises to make you feel more energised, look more supple, smell more vibrant and appear more relevant. For the city that produces nothing but images, words and stories - the glamorous life of the celebrity is the focus for all of these myths. Indeed, it would appear the old Gods from Olympus still walk among us, but now they all star in reality TV shows, and do a lucrative magazine deal for their wedding photos.

In today's pantheon Aphrodite works a red carpet in Balenciaga couture.

The youth wield the power, so we are told, and we are obsessed with the young and the beautiful. School teachers moan and old farts berate the fact that old people have become quite peripheral. So the kids with ambrosial locks cut their hair into wild swathes of freedom. London thrives on good hair.

I love this place, yet I'm leaving because in my heart it feels that I am done. I'm tired of all of this.

Transitions.

Changes.

Clothes left in attics of friend's houses leave me feeling so much lighter. I am reinvigorated and thirsty for a new phase in my life; like a pagan ritual, I have given up dying my hair and instead I shave my head. I feel so much lighter. I run my hands across the stubble and the sensation is exhilarating.

I wonder if it is this time of year that makes me think like this? Or perhaps it is this town? Clapham is a place that in it's gentrification seems to have forgotten that it actually belongs in zone 2 of a sprawling metropolis. It's become a beautiful town that behaves like a quaint country village; complete with an annual village fete full of cows. To me it feels like the place has evolved into a pastiche of something that once appeared on the cover of a box of shortbread. I remember this used to be the town where you could get a decent E and a blow job anywhere on the common after dark. I doubt very much that is the case now, my how things have changed. The only thing you can score on the common these days is a friendly game of cricket.

Clapham high street is littered with young, fresh Antipodean immigrants, men full of rugby who exude the prevailing sense that they would prefer to live in Chelsea. Sometimes it smells of disappointment, even though today is a wonderful September day, I loathe to be in Clapham.

Drinks with Jay doesn't help my melancholy. It alleviates my feelings of inadequacy for a while; but soon they are back and like the craggy lines of a darkened hangover, these thoughts shred apart my day. I always feel quite shit when I'm with Jay, it's not him, it's me.

I joke about my mid-life crisis. Why not? I bear witness to the many eccentricities adopted by men my age who live in complete denial. I see men with young girlfriends and ludicrous cars that are sporty. Some men run to the sunbeds in memory of holidays gone by when they felt that they ruled the world. Mostly they become orange and look rather creepy, I can't help thinking that this will be Jay's path in life, he's always loved his holidays in Sitges. I'm pretty sure Jay wants to get married. He's one step away from a husband in Brighton and a sunny retirement full of cats.

Jason is always referred to as *"Jay"* and he is, by all accounts, rather irritating. Gregarious, ostentatious and vain; he has a knack of charming girls who find his bitchy, camp posturing good fun. According to his Gaydar profile:

1. - He is "*down to earth and friendly*"
2. - He hates men who are "up-themselves"
3. - He loves going on "holiday" and hates people who "travel,"
4. - He wants a "normal" man who is "straight acting" and "down to earth,
5. - His favourite food is "sushi."
6. - He is "27" years old.

How much of this is true I can't really say; I have never seen him eat sushi, and I distinctly remember being invited to his 27th birthday party several years ago. It was a gaudy fake-tan and big hair affair held at an extremely over-priced west-end hotel.

We are all complicit in our fictions.

No, despite his protestations to the contrary, Jay is nothing like his Grindr profile; but in his defense, it is something to which he aspires, in his eyes it makes him seem more interesting. To some degree I think that's slightly more tragic than me once dying my hair; but I suppose essentially it's all the same thing.

Since becoming more successful as a hair stylist, Jay has secured his position in London gay society and he has taken steps to ensure that his grooming is always "fashion," without looking too "try hard." The fake tan is now less severe, more subtle and expensive and the clothes are at the very least, *'All Saints,'* no more *'Top-man'* for Jay: He has made it in this town, and everything worth anything is "fabulous!"

He likes my new hair and complements my look; apparently the salt and pepper grey makes me look more, "*distinguished;*" whether or not I AM more, "distinguished," doesn't even matter, I look "*distinguished;*" So therefore I am.

Despite all this, I find his company seductively entertaining and his gossipy stories of celebrity clients never fail to make me laugh. In a way we are the same; duplicitous lives lived in a town full of smoke and mirrors. He brandishes his camp, Manchester accent like a blade, delivering his tales with such relish; secure in the knowledge that he is the one, down to earth, and everyone else is a fraud. He is working class and proud, and everything that does not fit his staunch view of, "normal," is labeled "pretentious," or, "mad." He finds nothing in the world that challenges the authenticity of a staunch northern upbringing.

His voice travels louder with every Mojito and against the background of South African barks and rugger-bugger drones, his northern grate is embellished with an air of camp credibility. Here among the recruitment consultants and the human resource managers, his points of view take on a sharply world-wise exoticism; in fact he is totally engrossing and unique. There are many successful people in London who describe themselves as, "Working class," but so few of them actually are.

Here, Jay exaggerates his insecurities and so becomes a triumphant representation of individuality, a native amid the ex-pats. I often wonder what actually defines Jay as, "working class?" His accent? His insistence on trumpeting the principles of socialist ideology while sipping fine Champagne? No, it is his past, not his present or his future that gives him the right to be condescending towards the people who, in his mind, once made him feel small. In a city that sells elegance as a lifestyle choice, a hairdresser is crucial; he has worked his advantage, and now he revels in his success.

I think this is why I like him so much. We both have a difficult relationship with our homes and our pasts, and such silly trauma's manifest themselves in the oddest of ways, yet we made a niche for ourselves here among the millionaires and the mad men.

As usual he holds court with women of a certain age and today is no exception.

There's a thirty something, blond make-up artist from Kent who now lives in Clapham and works for an exorbitantly expensive cosmetics company based in Sloane square. She hates anything that looks cheap and has, over the years, honed the difficult skill of being obnoxious to anyone who enters her boutique not suitably attired in this seasons look. She cannot abide women who, "let themselves go," despite the fact that at the moment she is a great advocate of, "the natural look." This is a look which seems to involve spending a vast amount of time and money on products and preparations that keep her looking natural and young. This irony is lost on her.

Her name is Jo. Although; it doesn't really matter what her name is because, like everyone at this prestigious table, Jay has introduced them as either, "love," or, "darling." We are all getting very drunk. It is a sunny September Sunday and everyone is all about the Mojito.

Then there is Carly from New Zealand, she is an artist, she seems thoughtful and pensive and has the air of belonging to a different table. She observes rather than becomes involved. It is this subtle mystique that lends her a fascinating attractiveness, is that it? Perhaps she is just hungover or embarrassed by Jays bludgeoning conversational anecdotes? Whatever her reasons for remaining quietly attentive, yet safely at a distance, she fascinates me the most. Her hair is jet and sculpted tight into an asymmetrical shape that is the mark of a true individual. She belongs in Dalston.

Beside Jo sits Marianne, a lady in her early thirties who works as a sub-editor for a Sunday supplement celebrity magazine. She is a successful career woman, her magazine has a distribution of millions and it has been said that a nod from her at a fashion show will have all the girls hemlines disappearing or dangling in an instant. She likes to think of herself as a south London Anna Wintour. All of these rumours are spread by her; one wonders just how much clout a sub-editor wields, but regardless of the boasting and bragging, she has achieved a position and respect hitherto unthinkable for a woman as little as 40 years ago.

I like her boasting, but sometimes I feel it's compensatory, why?

Well, being the gossipy queen that he is, Jay has told me on numerous occasions of her broken down cocaine mornings and her desire for a family. Does the opportunity to have it all mean that she should get nothing? Why do I feel there is a moral obligation to her story? Despite all the talk of progress there are still different expectations on men and women. Her success would be a smaller mans failure, it's almost like her place in history is limited and like every woman before her she should be mindful of her home and compartmentalise each role. She should be an actress in her own personal domestic scene.

It is clear to me she runs the show. She feigns submission and allows her boss to think he is the boss, this is part of her greatness. She willingly plays a part in his success and like a puppeteer she performs but is not seen.

All of these women are single and this, so I have been told, is a particularly modern phenomenon. I wonder just how true this is, hasn't this always been the case? Surely Women have always been widows or wives or mothers or single, they have found company with their friends at tables full of heartbreak and laughter. They bolster each other, for theirs is a life full of disappointments. It is this acquiescence that enables them a true enjoyment of the moment. Why should they concern themselves with the fictions of men? The day to day for them can be problematic, I don't know. I will be the first to admit that women have always been a mystery to me. A simple conversation about hair is never simple; it is brimming with subtext.

Jay is currently enthralling his audience with the latest gossip about his new client, the infamous "Keeley." She is a contemporary so notorious she can exist in the public consciousness without a surname. Despite her publicist's desperate attempts to give credence to her literary endeavours by re-branding her as the much more wholesome and agreeable, "Keeley Singleton;" she will always be known to the public as just, "*that slapper Keeley.*"

. . . . . . . . . . . . . . .

I feel like I am on the set of a weary episode of *Sex in the City,* the camera's are turned off and the crew are busy thinking of a sales pitch. It feels like each woman at this table is an actor playing an authentic characterisation of the modern woman, but it can only be realised by a fabulously hammy performance.

Perhaps I project too much? Nobody at this table performs in social situations more than Jay or I.

Apparently every woman must suffer, I think sometimes in England we adore the suffrage of others, we are the champions of misery. I hate the fact that so many women justify their work by cultivating an aura of sacrifice. What is this life? It is lived and experienced with blood and bone but painted with a frivolous mask that shimmers. Women live every horror that we men can only imagine or replicate with violence and war, we remain eternally the compensatory sex, and yes they talk of hair.

As Jay begins to narrate the story of Keeley, the women are engrossed and bulging with opinions. It would appear that women are their own worst critics, for Keeley can do nothing right. Jay entertains us by assuming her accent and mimicking her trademark traits. He mimes her affectations with such precision that we are lost in his performance, in the tradition of story-tellers gone by, we feel that Keeley is among us.

It transpires that Keeley is currently presiding over a carefully orchestrated media circus to promote her latest ghost-penned autobiography, "*From Pain to Gain*." It appears Ms Singleton's publicist has had the brilliance to tap into the lucrative misery memoir market. This ingenious concept manages to marry both her tragic life, and her ongoing obsession with weight-loss. "*From Pain to Gain*," is a follow up to her first tome, "*Show Me on the Dolly where the Bad Man Touched You*," an autobiography so mind-bogglingly morose that it became an instant bestseller in the UK. Hence Keeley was instantaneously elevated from the status of mere *WAG*, to the dizzying heights of *National Treasure*. Don't worry if you don't understand all of these terms, suffice to say there are varying degrees of celebrity only evident to people who work in the industry. Keeley is rich, always in the news and utterly shameless, which puts her way above a simple girl-band member.

I had the misfortune of having to read, "*Show Me on the Dolly where the Bad Man Touched You*," in order to review it for an expat magazine in Berlin. My editor described it as, "dreck," and then asked me if everyone who was working class in England had been abused and maltreated? I assured him that this was an exceptional case; he then pointed to an episode of the, "*Jeremy Kyle Show*," that was showing on the satellite TV station. I remember being uncomfortably ashamed of being poor and white and British.

"*Show Me on the Dolly where the Bad Man Touched You*," was such a monumentally tragic piece of prose that I was instantly stunned into a bitter disillusion with the human race. This is a massive failure on the part of everyone involved. I found it nearly impossible to review such a piece, even in my darkest days, I had never experienced such vile disenchantment. Maybe it has been exaggerated? In my heart I hope it has, but even then, if it has been embellished for reasons of publication then why on earth would anyone wish to immerse themselves in such a hideous life?

Keeley's career has been defined by the men in her life, and like any heroine of a tale of triumph over adversity, she is always a victim at the mercy of some cruel man who enjoys her beauty and then rapes her of her innocence. It's a savage and brutal tale, yet she finds the strength to persevere; to leave home, to find work as a hostess, then to marry - happily ever after? No, first to a striker from Grimsby town FC, who has been relegated to a paragraph in the early chapters of her life. Husband number two was a premier league player, with this promotion she was elevated to the dazzling heights of being a battered wife. This is a story that almost celebrates misogyny with every blunt and brutal anecdote, it does nothing but affirm her passive complicity. Who are these people?

Have these men in her life forgotten their grandmothers who had worked and bled to build the blitzed out homes of our civilisation? Probably, it is so much more appealing to remember your grandfather who had died for his country, far away in some foreign land, than it is to acknowledge the shit left behind. I know that all too often history forgets the wives and mothers who are destined to become faceless cleaners. They are the scrubbers who exist to polish up their little soldiers to prepare them for an honourable, celebrated death or, at the very least, a career as a first division wife beater.

This is Sunday, the day before work, and no-one wishes to think of such depressing things. On this particular Sunday the glamour under discussion is not a valiant death for Queen and country - no - we are all engrossed in the equally engaging topic of whether a fringe will make Keeley Singleton appear more intellectual.

According to Jay her current hair extensions make her look, "a right stupid fuckin cow..." and, "common as muck!" This may seem trivial, but in order to sell the books, to make the money, to pay the countless people who depend upon this industry for a living, the question of a fringe employs some gravitas. A multitude of people have invested time and energy in brand, "*Keeley,*" and are reliant upon its success - She must appear relevant. In many ways it all hangs on the bangs, as the Americans might say.

Regardless of who she really is, the image of Keeley must convey something aspirational, she must be desirable.

Jo says "yes," and bleats that anything is better than her current do.

- "All those fake extensions make her look like a right slag, but then again I suppose she is."

Jo hates Keeley with a passion, and with an elegant swish, she swipes her honey-blond locks behind her shoulders and protrudes her perfectly moisturised chin. It's hard for me to replicate her venom, but it seems she thinks that Keeley is "A slapper," "an embarrassing little slut," who "gives every woman a terrible name!" In many ways I have to agree.

Just how Keely's hair designates her relationships with men I shall never know. I have always imagined Keeley to be anything but sexually promiscuous, despite all the exaggerated posturing and seductive posing. She mimes sexual availability and yet at the same time she somehow manages to seem totally unprovocative.

With a belly full of beer I convince myself that she is exactly the opposite of sexy and I picture rather awkward scenarios filled with frigid fumbling, limp proclamations of pleasure, and rhythmless gyrations. Altogether the whole experience would amount to a cold and uninspiring coupling, hardly incendiary.

Marianne is less enraged by Keeley but allows herself a giggle at Jo's animated response. Much more pragmatic, she appears to see the bigger picture and touches her face with a nod of contemplation.

- "I don't know, the big hair is her thing, I mean, what is her key demographic?"

It is clear to me that Marianne has carved out a successful career for herself by utilising such buzz phrases as, *"key demographic."* I've no idea what it means, but then again, I'm not a successful business woman.

Jay clarifies the situation for me by answering:

- "Well you're looking at Lorraine Kelly's audience, and your 'Loose women,' basically it's teenage girls who are knocked up and dried up old bags... You know...Women without a fuckin job!"

He's drunk of course, and this is not the case, but hidden among the scathing remarks I find my question answered. It's all about the marketing.

- "I showed her what the fringe would look like and her stupid fucking assistant, who's a right fucking bitch, reckons it would make her look too old fashioned. OLD FASHIONED! I mean she's wearing a vintage frock for fuck sake. I said it would all be really, really nice... You know like, 1950's American rockabilly chic which is, like, REALLY hot right now... So fuckin' stylish yeah, 'specially with that dress; and that cow of an assistant was like, 'it's not really Keeley, can you glam it up a bit?' Stupid fuckin' bitch."

He gurns a look of total disgust this is all genuinely amusing.

I'm not calling Jay a liar, but I know him well enough to know that in his work environment, he is the epitome of diplomatic efficiency. He flatters and expresses his opinion but ultimately he adheres to the will of the client. He knows just how far to take his creative integrity; and he also knows just how to get his own way and still get paid. Today we are privy to the venting of his passive aggressive bile and to some degree I feel I'm rather privileged. Apparently "Fringe-gate," as Carly has rather wryly called it, has ensured that the shoot is to continue on Monday. None of the images are suitable, and now Keeley's assistant wants to try another shoot and needs the time to consider the possibility of a fringe with her management team.

Everything hangs on those bangs...

- "Well maybe the fringe is a bit too much Jay...I mean, for Christ sake you have to break them in gently! She's been falling out of clubs in heels, and sloshing about in velour tracksuits for the past six years,"

slurs Marianne.

- "Falling out of her dress more like, those tits of hers are shocking...Even when she was in that beautiful, vintage frock her stylist was pinning it and pushing up the tits! That dress had more pricks than I've had in a lifetime! It's totally fucked."

It would appear she is truly our Keeley, every person that buys her endorsed products or her books has an opinion about her, she is owned by anyone and everyone. We've witnessed every high and low, and now that she is public property she has no private life, every part of her tragic existence is carefully scripted by PR and fed to an awaiting maelstrom of glossy mags and talk-shows. Without her media profile she is nothing. She is no-one. I am confused and drunk and baffled by it all. Is this what little girls really dream about? Is this what Keeley wanted? Is she really living the dream? Was there ever a moment when a young girl looked at her mother and wept, "*when I grow up, I want to have a nervous breakdown in public.*"

Perhaps she needs a fringe, it would suit her best - something behind which she can hide...

Just a minute.

Sorry my friends, I have become somewhat distracted and appear to be projecting a favourable impression of this women. How do I know anything about her? I only met her once and reviewed a book to which she put her name; she didn't even write it. She could be awful for all I know, in which case I've been hoodwinked by her PR machine. Am I just a drunken fool who has been duped to care about someone who does not need my sympathy?

She's the working class girl made good by selling out her self respect and pandering to the populace. Good for her! She's rich and exploited and we all know life is so much easier with money. I shudder when I think about her, and her hair, why have we spent the last hour discussing her fucking hair?

Do I really give a fuck about her hair?

Jo and Marianne cackle and laugh as Jay performs his pantomime Keeley with exaggerated misery, and he pads out his show with ridiculous one liners. At our table this afternoon, she's a thick Northern bitch who manipulates and dominates and bumbles through her perfect life without a conscience.

For a moment, it's all too vile for me; I am overcome with guilt at spending my Sunday revelling in Keeley's tragic experiences. However, it's just so deliciously entertaining.

Why?

Why the fuck should I care about anything that Keeley has to say? Why is she even on my radar? In a flash I can remember there was that time she found her Father dead; he had died as a result of a bizarre auto-asphyxiation accident. He had wanked himself to death. He was a definite fore-runner to the trend, some might say he was ahead of his time, in more ways than one. He remains in our hearts the Godfather of the embarrassing death. I ask Jay if Keeley mentions the incident in her latest book. Apparently she does, but she claims it was an unfortunate accident. Apparently he tripped and fell in the bathroom and his trousers ended up around his ankles; while at the same time, his belt somehow managed to get caught in the door and strangle him.

True, I suppose, it could happen to anyone. There's always an element of tragedy attached to death by, '*asphyxie-wank,*' but for Jay, Jo, Marrianne, and myself on a boozy Sunday in Clapham this is fair game. We are rolling around laughing.

I have considered the peculiarities of women but I cannot escape the fact that there are men in the world that actually wank themselves to death.

What am I doing here? *I really don't belong in this girls sorry life, why do I know anything about her?* Why am I here?

I cannot blame the drink this time, something has shifted. Something that I cannot quite vocalise, but it's a deep hatred of my London life. I feel restless and unsatisfied and in my heart I know that I've been at this table for far too long.

. . . . . . . . . . . . . .

It seems that Carly understands me.

She quietly looks around and smiles at the company with a graceful resolve that is reassuring. She looks at me with a knowing shimmer in her eyes and I feel the most profound empathy. I am calmed by her presence. She identifies my foolish turmoil; lifting her head she says to the table with a subtle confident reserve,

- "I totally think you should go with the fringe doll..."

# PART 1 – DALSTON – AUGUST – 2010

- "Coz you know me Tell... I ain't a racial-ist..."
- "I know Jean."
- "I serve em all in here."
- "Tha's right Jean yeah..."
- "And I love my Tyrone. He's a good boy, not like his Dad but still..."
- "Course Jean, yeah"
- "...But some of them black kids is out running round all night, no wonder they're all stabbin each other. It ain't safe for 'em to be walkin the streets that time of night..."
- "Tha's right Jean yeah..."

Apparently Jeanette was a looker in her day, but in this particular scene, she looks like she's a character being played by Sir Ian Mckellen.

Naturally he would have to bulk up for the role, but the facial resemblance is uncanny. Punters who have been barred refer to her as, "*the pterodactyl lady.*" She's stocky and hard, yet she moves with a grace that betrays her beautiful past. She wipes and she cleans, she always has a cloth in her hand. She, "puts the world to rights."

This is her world.

Terry props up the bar. He was a postman, but now he does the bins in town. It takes him an hour to get to work. He works for people who don't see him, cleaning streets on which he can't afford to live. Most days he can be found here, in the pub, propping up the bar. He drinks pale ale and smokes roll ups. Every now and then he likes a shot of Irish whiskey.

- "Still no word about Tyrone Jean?"
- "No Tell. Tanya's down there now... I ain't heard nothin."
- "Tanya all right is she?"
- "No Terence. She's not alright. She's been worried sick... Ain't you 'eard a word I've said?"

You leave them to their conversation and head to the table by the fruit machine near the bar. The table is covered with yesterdays news.

Yesterdays news isn't good. Yesterdays news is a crumpled up picture of flowers by a railing and suddenly you feel disenchanted, disillusioned. It appears you have been abandoned by the stories that once gave you comfort and hope. This is not your world, your life, you are not a part of this. It surrounds you with despair. You have a right to be cynical. You've grown accustomed to detachment. You know these people, these lives, you are local of course but you keep to yourself.

You consider the Olympic logo which everyone thinks is shit. It is random shapes and objects forced together at a tangent and you wonder how it fits together on the page? It's just so uncomfortably ugly.

- "He'll be all right Jean... Your Tyrone's a good boy..."
- "I know he's a good boy but they don't know that! As far as they're concerned he's mixed race with previous... They don't care."

This pub is your local, but for some reason you wouldn't call it that. It is faded, but Jean keeps it fastidiously clean. It has the odour of lock-in cigarettes and cheap furniture polish. You know the lives of many of the regulars, and as it's a Saturday evening you know later it will be packed. There's already a few familiar faces.

Directly opposite you, bug eyed and sinking pints, is the rock band, "*The Fucking Cunts.*" The lead singer Bill O'Callaghan, whose real name is William Goldsmith, has a bragging swagger and he gulps down chunks of cheap lager. He is surrounded by a harem of girls who wear skinny jeans. Terry's gruff voice interjects your observations...

- "...Don't get yourself in a state Jean... If he ain't done nothin, then he ain't done nothin. Simple as that..."

And Jean wipes the drip-treys in silence.

You focus on the band. You like their music. Their debut album, *"SPUNK JUNKIES,"* had some really great tracks, it received 5 stars from 'Q' magazine who described it as, *"seminal."* Evidently, Bill O'Callaghan is the new peoples poet. He refers to himself as an artist; he has an ex-council flat just down the road where he entertains all the painfully hip and perpetually wasted. You know his stylist, she tells you the truth. She tells you he lives at his girlfriend's house in Primrose hill. She gives you all the gossip because these stories help relieve the boredom.

Apparently his mother, Mrs Goldsmith, lives in Sussex by the sea and she tells his Grand-mama that he works in entertainment. Young William Goldsmith used to play cricket and collect shells from the beach. William Goldsmith loved the beach and the open spaces; he once dreamed of being a famous pirate. Bill O'callaghan collects tattoo's and embarrassing venereal diseases; mainly crabs, and he talks with a cock-er-nee chirp about, "football," and "birds." The band are recording their difficult second album, in a studio just off Kingsland road, by all accounts it's not going too well.

Most days they are to be found in here pissed.

With your first pint finished you are imbued with a new confidence and feel invigorated by a sense of release. You shouldn't feel so alienated. Though you cannot really afford another beer, it has been the sort of day when another beer is all that you require. Today was another rubbish job interview. You are exhausted from persuading men you don't like to give you a job that you'd hate; selling things you don't care about, to people who don't need them. You feel you are just passing through. You head to the bar and stand next to Terry. He views you slightly skewed and takes a pensive sip.

- "Ain't that that Blossom Malone over there?"

He nods towards *"The Fucking Cunts,"* and following his gesture sure enough, you view the feted celebrity mess to which he refers. Blossom Malone sits gauchely with her arm draped over a curly haired boy who is trying too hard. Blossom Malone drinks pints of cider with ice, but you've heard she prefers Krug Champagne. She describes herself as a, "model/presenter," and her Dad was a famous pop-star who made his name at that big charity gig; so, you've seen her grow up in all the crap magazines. She's a complete mess, lost in the media fiction, to many she is aspirational, some even call her an inspiration.

- "She ain't bad in real life... When you see her on the telly she looks like she's got a face like a bag of spanners."

Poor Blossom Malone you think to yourself. She appears to have everything but it's all a facade, and she can't even manage a suicide - she's failed both times - and for a second you wonder why you know her? Why do you know her and not the boy who lived down the road? The boy whose face lies crumpled in yesterdays news.

- "Face like a bag'a'spanners! HA!... I ain't heard that in years...Terry you do make me die!"

Jean is interrupted by a vibration from her mobile phone, followed by an ever increasing ring-tone loop of the *Boney-M'* track, *Ma Baker*. She seems unsettled, and picking up her mobile phone she hands it across the bar to Terry.

- "Now how do I make this work again Tell? I can't make it work."
- "Give it here...You're doing it all wrong... You just press this one here see..."

- "Cheers Tell... Hello?... Hello? Oh alright love yeah... No I can't hear nothing, one sec, I'll take you out the back, Terry can you watch the bar a sec while I talk to Tanya? Karen's running late."

Terry nods and Jean disappears through an open doorway and into the kitchen, a mysterious place where many seem to enter but only doorstep sandwiches leave. Terry doesn't move his bulky frame, he continues the relentless task of supping ale, it is his reason for being. He always seems surly, but today he's particularly serious.

- "That'll be about the boy. He ain't got nothing to do with it, he's harmless, wouldn't hurt a fly."

You feel like you are eavesdropping. This is not your world, so you perch and you drink and you look around for another distraction.

The old rockabilly boys are sitting at a table sipping stout. They are playing here tonight, having finished their sound-check, they're killing time playing cards and drinking. They live in a vintage world with their slick quiffs and turn-ups, they met at their work in the Job-center. They call themselves musicians, and only like authentic rock and roll. They play roadhouse blues and old skiffle tunes, which Bradley (double-bass) considers the only true music. Bradley spends his money on a classic Chevrolet which has a tendency to break down at round-a-bouts. Like many of his friends, he fashions a nostalgic life which, strangely, isn't out of place among the shell-suits and the trainers. Everyone seeks authenticity. The band are quite swinging; they draw a quirky crowd of plumbers in braces and ladies who rock that whole fifties thing.

With a flurry and a jangle of cheap jewelry, Karen enters the pub. She's laden with hoodies, brollies and plastic bags. She is blushed and scrubbed. She moves with a confident ease, she has purpose in her world.

- "Sorry I'm late Tell, I had to drop off Shanice at Sharon's coz Aisha's going down the carnival and she's already looking after Marika... Anyway... Jean out the back?"
- "Alright Kazza... Yeah... She's out the back."
- "Any news?"
- "She's on the phone to Tanya now..."

The door flings open, some blue suits wearing casuals barge in. They bray like donkeys. Everyone thinks they're cunts. It's their day off and they've been, "on it," since 10 o'clock this morning. They live in the gated new build by Middleton road and they work in the city. Dave is their ring-leader. Apparently he has "bollocks," and can chat up the "skirt." Dave describes himself as a "right cunt," and apparently this is a good thing. He blunders through the floor to the bar, barking away at anyone and everyone, because they all need to know what he thinks. He calls this pub a "fuckin' shit-hole," yet he is in here most days.

It must be raining again because people trickle in sprinkled with water. Following Dave and his herd come Peter and Cameron. Peter is red haired and round with a skin head covered by a baseball cap, he has perfectly sculpted, short, ginger lamb-chop sideburns. At times he reminds you of a particularly hairy pumpkin. He made his money in the 1980's shooting video porn in Soho but he gave that up. He says it was because of all the pretentious queens in Soho but, you think it's because he failed to foresee the impact of the Internet. Now he lives locally installing cable networks into people's houses. He Likes Cameron, but he cannot stand "poofy" gays.

Cameron isn't really called "Cameron" because he is from Thailand. Peter met him on holiday and gave him his new name and then married him. Cameron is willowy, golden and serene and comes across as quite passive. He smiles a face full of joy and always appears graceful. Peter likes to tell you all of his secret fetishes, possibly to shock you. He considers himself a socialist; however, he fantasises about buggering pretty, preppy ex-public schoolboys. He calls them "bear-bait" and "posh-cubs." Subsequently, he often likes to dress Cameron up in a blazer and bum him over their breakfast bar. During sex he loves to shout, "take that Cameron you dirty little bitch!" He feels this is his two fingered salute to the Tory party. Cameron smiles and studies computer engineering.

The bar is filling up now and Karen is rushing around in the work zone. She keeps hurried and focused on her work. She likes her job, she even finds time for a kind word, and chats to everyone waiting at the bar. Dave the cunt is between you and Pete, buying a round for, what seems like everyone in the pub and he barks his estuary bleat; you really don't want to know what he thinks - it's not your world - but you just can't help it. You're sucked in.

- "... Fanks Karen love and two more Jack Daniels and cokes and two more pints of lager... Tell you what mate... Took me over a fucking hour to get back yesterday from a meeting. Fucking tube drivers on strike! I mean - firtie fuckin grand a year they get for sittin on their arses all fuckin day, Firtie grand! I mean they get paid more than nurses..."

At first you think that Pete is intimidated by Dave, but then of course you realise that he is viewing him with utter contempt. It seems Dave is the red rag to Pete's bull. Word to the wise, you think to yourself, never wheel out the nurses argument in front of Pete. It's a whole can of worms.

- "Everyone gets paid more than nurses. I bet you get paid more than nurses. Why not just pay the nurses more? "

His wings are clipped but Dave is still flying, he's not used to being confronted because, in his world, he is always right. For a moment he flounders like a gutted mullet in a Billingsgate bin. He straightens up his blue, Fred Perry short sleeved shirt; his hands instinctively play with a missing tie, and so prepared for battle he says:

- "Course I earn more than the nurses, I should earn more than the nurses. I'm an important financial cog in the wheel of the national economy..."

Pete reddens more and Cameron squeezes his shoulder.

You order one more pint from Karen, it appears in front of you with a jangle of gold just in time to see Jean reappear behind the bar.

Is that a smile or does she have wind?

Something about her seems lighter and flushed as she takes up her cloth with renewed vigour. She puffs up with pride and parades around her bar - her world - for she is the queen. The noise around the bar swells with laughter as more and more people take refuge from the showers. They carve out a tight space in this dysfunctional home from home. Terry stiffly leans forward over the sodden bar cloths and shouts at Jean. She glides over to your end of the bar.

- "Any news?"
- "Yeah. They say he had nothin' to do with it, which is what I was saying all along. I'm gonna kill 'im though... You'll never guess where he was..."
- "Go on..."
- "He was round that bloody Chantelle's, Tha's why he didn't say nothin'... I'll bloody kill him"
- "What you talking about? She's a cracking little bird. You should be happy that he didn't have nothing to do with all that bloody drama!"
- "I know that, but I can't stand her... Saucy mare."
- "How's Tanya?"
- "She's over the moon, she'll be back any minute; apparently she says she went up there, an' the headmaster was there with the police and everything. All of them said the same. She says that they all said that Tyrone's a good boy, and he knew of the other boy but they weren't never friends or nothink. Course Tanya, being just like me, says she turns round and says to them, "What made you think it was my Tyrone?" and the Sergent says, he

says, “Tyrone fitted the description of someone in the area,” so Tanya says, she says, “yeah whats that then? Black?” I nearly died!”

- “Come on now Jean calm it down. No need for that. End’a’tha’day there’s still some poor kiddie that’s died. Show some respect will ya... End’a’tha’day Jean... Someones’s dead”

Tenderly she reaches over and strokes the back of his broad hand; she is genuinely moved by her old friend's compassion and sense of honour and respect. You can see his words have an impact her face betrays, for a moment, her grief at someone's loss.

- “You’re right Tell... Imagine being that poor sods mother. She’ll be going through the mill I bet... poor cow.”

It’s true you think to yourself. How can you empathise with something so brutal?

You’ve overheard enough and this is not your life, or your world. You feel momentarily like you are on the set of some badly written soap opera; a terribly orchestrated pastiche of working class life in London. You think about drinking up and leaving.

Just in time, Tanya bangs the wooden doors open and sweeps into the lounge bar. She is beautiful and exudes a natural elegance and charm. She has long dark hair that is tousled without affectation, and she’s slender but she’s healthy. When she was younger she was harder, more brittle and sharp. She demanded without a conscience; she wanted Tyrone more than anything - more than Tyrone’s father. Now she has softened and is open to accept things as they are. With her comes relief, relief that today is not the day when the world crumbles. Today is her day to celebrate her son’s good fortune.

At once there’s a moment of clarity.

The picture achieves cohesion. She brings together all the fragments and the broken tales and suddenly the story has relevance. She flutters around with a kind word for everyone and anyone, she knows them all. You look around and realise you are as much a part of this room as anyone else. You are one of many stranger friends who live their lives here, separate entities yet intrinsically linked. Tanya instinctively knows our failures and our triumphs, our loses and our lucky gains. Today she counts herself among the lucky ones.

She goes over to *“The Fucking Cunts,”* who all cheer. Bill O’Callaghan stands and you are sure you catch a glimpse of William Goldsmith; not the affected pout for cameras, the gentle smile of good nature. He momentarily relinquishes his music hall drawl. He hugs her and seems to be genuinely sharing her happiness. “That’s fantastic news

Tanya, I'm really pleased for you." Blossom Malone shakes free of the skinny boy and hugs her, she even manages a smile. She then rushes out to vomit up her cider.

Next stop in her infectious whirl, Tanya greets the men at the bar; first there is Cameron, he timidly tips his head and smiles, he says he is pleased for her news. He thinks Tyrone is funny. They share the same taste in computer games. He offers to fix Tyrone's laptop, then he gently touches Peter's shoulder. Tanya looks tiny next to Pete, they look like a scene from a victorian fable. He peers down to smile at her and says, "Alright girl," and he scoops her up engulfing her in the biggest of bear hugs. She looks like a modern day Goldilocks, with brown hair and more jewellery.

She is illuminating and everyone can connect with her story. It is genuine and even Dave calls her "princess," he offers to buy her a drink. It's a fairytale scene with a boorish commodity broker smashed on cocaine instead of a prince. As usual he says what he thinks, "...It's a fucking liberty that Tyrone was called on in the first place!" At this point you lose all interest in what he is saying.

For just a moment the dead belong to yesterdays news, the living breathe today.

Once again your mind conjures up that contentious Olympic logo. Maybe it does make some sense. Then again, maybe you're drunk. However misshapen and clunky it appears, perhaps the parts do belong together and fit on the same page. There is lucidity in the language evoked by that symbol, though it is incongruous.

Tanya is at the bar drinking white wine and soda with Terry, as the old boys in the band begin to play. They play old tunes that are worn-in and familiar and everyone knows them. The young and the old, the rich and the poor, all sing the same songs. Everyone's drinking and dancing as she reaches out and softly touches your waist. You don't belong here but then again perhaps that means that you do. You might try to pretend that you are not of this world but you are, you just need to find your place. You realise that your time has come; so you surrender to the intoxication of the moment and prepare to be embraced.

It's in moments like these that we live dear to each other; whether we remain here or like the Olympic athletes who exceed all expectations and cross frontiers in order to achieve their triumphs, we all eventually receive our rewards. What is the point of all this? What is the ultimate reward? I have no idea what I'm looking for, but I know it will be fine; both in this life, and in the pilgrimage of a thousand years that has been described by more eloquent men than me.

I think it's time to see the world.

# ABOUT THE AUTHOR

MrE has worked professionally in the entertainment industry for many years. Now he works as a part-time lecturer, teacher and travelling boffin. He remains single, unmarried and unashamedly romantic.

He writes for the love of writing.

Sometimes he wishes he had stayed at home, but the world is just too big.

5980784R00079

Printed in Great Britain
by Amazon.co.uk, Ltd.,
Marston Gate.